Howard T. Crocket.
1868 Gaylord St,
Denver.
Colo.

SHADOWS OF THE STAGE

SECOND SERIES

SHADOWS OF THE STAGE

SECOND SERIES

WILLIAM WINTER

Author of "Shakespeare's England"

"Come like shadows, so depart"
— Shakespeare

MACMILLAN AND CO.

SHADOWS OF THE STAGE

SECOND SERIES

BY

WILLIAM WINTER

AUTHOR OF "SHAKESPEARE'S ENGLAND"

"Come like shadows — so depart"
SHAKESPEARE

New York
MACMILLAN AND COMPANY
AND LONDON
1893

Norwood Press:
J. S. Cushing & Co. — Berwick & Smith.
Boston, Mass., U.S.A.

TO

Edwin Booth

HONOURING A NOBLE CHARACTER

A GENTLE AND BENEFICENT LIFE

A FINE DRAMATIC GENIUS

AND AN ILLUSTRIOUS CAREER

THESE MEMORIALS

OF SOME OF HIS CONTEMPORARIES

ARE AFFECTIONATELY INSCRIBED

PREFACE.

———◆———

It is perhaps to be regretted that the note of censure makes itself audible in this volume. It is easy to utter blame: it is difficult, and much better, to utter intelligent and thoughtful praise. Certain subjects, however, which must be treated, if theatrical history is to be written, can only be treated in one way. The life of Forrest, for example, cannot be excluded from the theatrical record, and it cannot be justly recounted without censure. The presence of foreign schools of acting cannot be ignored, and assuredly the irrational claims that are made in their behalf ought to be met with an occasional word of protest. In the face of wayward innovations the plea for reason and simplicity is always appropriate. No word has been written in an unjust spirit. The subjects discussed have prompted the method of their discussion. The purpose is mainly

7

*commemorative and historical. This vol-
ume, like its predecessor, is composed of
essays of mine collected from The New York
Tribune and other periodicals to which I
have contributed during many years. The
record of dramatic achievement on the
American stage within the period of one
generation could be largely extended. An
effort has been made to include as much
as possible within a brief compass. Many
shining names and interesting subjects are
omitted, for want of space. A few of my
papers have, with consent, been reproduced
from the private prints of the Dunlap Society and from those of my friend Augustin
Daly. My essays on the Acting of Edwin
Booth are reserved for a separate volume
of this series.*

W. W.

March 12, 1892.

CONTENTS.

9

"*I'll be an auditor.*"   SHAKESPEARE.

———

"*Praise is a debt that we owe to the virtues of others.*"

SIR THOMAS BROWNE.

———

"*By the same aid the stage invites her friends,*
And kindly tells the banquet she intends;
Thither from real life the many run,
With Siddons weep and laugh with Abingdon;
Pleased in fictitious joy or grief to see
The mimic passion with their own agree;
To steal a few enchanted hours away
From self, and drop the curtain on the day."

CRABBE.

———

"*When an author dies it is no matter, for his works remain.   When a great actor dies there is a void produced in society, a gap which requires to be filled up.*"

HAZLITT.

———

"*The Glory and the Nothing of a Name.*"

BYRON.

SHADOWS OF THE STAGE.

———◆———

I.

THE RIGHT STANDARD.

CRITICISM is neither hostility nor scorn. The motive that impels a thoughtful observer to condemn much that is accepted by the multitude is not the wish merely to injure or to contemptuously deride or dismiss the popular mediocrity, but the desire that the age shall excel in all kinds of worth, and that the people shall both be the best and have the best. The poet Pope asserted the comfortable doctrine that "whatever is is right." Mr. Chalcote, the brewer, in Robertson's comedy of *Ours*, announced the freer though less agreeable conclusion, that "whatever is is wrong." There are writers who celebrate the glories of the present age, and who continually minister to vanity by informing the people that they are but little lower than the angels. Such writers are not the source of strength and help. The world does not prosper through being flattered. Too much is heard about the rights of man; too little about his duties. The moralists who frankly tell a people the truth, when that people, as often happens, is doing wrong and going wrong, are better friends of mankind than the flatterers of the popular mood and conduct.

Man is a brotherhood. In Roman days it was a saying with the aristocrats of mind and of rank, "the common people like to be deceived; deceived let them be." That saying was the essence of selfishness — a selfishness that the better part of the intellectual world has outgrown. There cannot be one law for persons of superior mental endowment and another law for the rest. Knowledge avails nothing unless it be communicated. Blessings are but half blessings if you keep them to yourself. Those who have clear vision and stalwart strength of mind should guide the rest of the world. The advancement of all human beings concerns every individual. The safety and comfort of the top of the pyramid depend on the security of the base. The enlightened philosopher knows that it is both self-interest and benevolence to keep the multitude in the right path — to civilise, to refine, to lead upward the masses of mankind, so that their eyes may be opened to beauty, their minds to truth, and their hearts to gentleness and aspiration. The guidance of the people is the duty of the thinker, and if he performs that duty he will sometimes speak in terms of censure, and he will make the censure positive enough to be felt and to be productive of good results.

Observation, with extended view, perceives that people in general are more deeply interested in what they call amusements than in serious occupations. You must study popular amusements, therefore, if you wish to understand the mental condition and tendency of the people. Those matters engross much attention, and it is through the discussion and guidance of their amusements that the people are most easily and directly reached and affected. Two methods of that discussion and guidance, both long in vogue, are sharply contrasted in contemporary practice — that of universal laudation, and that of objection and remonstrance. The former largely predominates, and it has wrought evil by making bad matters worse. Within recent years — although noble and beautiful works have been shown, and important steps have been taken — an avalanche of trash has been cast upon the stage, and the people have accepted it and have, practically, approved it, — while scarcely a voice among public censors has been raised against that flagrant abuse of the theatre. On the contrary, the public has been told to accept it, has been praised for accepting it, and has been prompted to encourage the extension of it. 'We are a hard-working, nervous, tired community' — so runs the stream of mischievous counsel — 'and we need recreation. When we go to the theatre we want to be amused. We do not want to think. Let us have something light!' Thus cajoled, and thus cajoling itself, the popular intelligence surrenders to folly, and the average theatrical manager brings forth *Rag Babies* and *Parlor Matches*, and complacently remarks, 'I must give them what they want.'

The writers and the managers who reason in that way do not reason well. It was unfortunate that the custom of viewing the stage as an "amusement" ever prevailed; for the stage is an institution higher and

finer than any amusement, and it possesses
an influence upon society second only to
that of the hearthstone. But, even viewing
it as one of the amusements, no man has a
right to degrade its character or impair its
usefulness. If we overwork ourselves, as a
community, let us quit that injurious and
useless custom. Half of the activity that
people commonly call "work" consists of
parade and pother. The actual work of
the world is done silently, by the minority, and usually it does not occupy all
the time or exhaust all the strength. Let
us economise our energies and stop the
snorting and the waste. If we are "tired"
and "nervous" we can, surely, rest and
refresh the nerves without turning the
stage into a playground for idiots and
making the theatre a hospital for victims
of dyspepsia. Sick persons are in no fit
condition to comprehend the drama, and
even if they were, the actor is not an
apothecary. The time for going to the play
is when you are well and refreshed and can
appreciate what you see and hear; when
your mind and soul are receptive and you
are not concerned with the state of your
stomach and the ills of your system. There
are influences in the dramatic art which can

ennoble and help you, even though they do
not foster the lower instincts or elicit va-
cant laughter.   The men and women who
devote their lives to the study and practice
of acting are not frivolous mountebanks,
emulous to make you laugh by cutting a
caper ; nor are you yourself such a poor
creature as you appear to be when you prat-
tle about your lassitude and allege your
preference for theatrical rubbish.

It is not meant that the stage is in a decline.   Ever since the theatre existed it has
been subject to fluctuations, accordant with
the moods and caprices of public taste.
There never has been a time in its history
when trash was not striving to submerge it,
and when base and sordid views of its province did not find specious advocates and
ignoble ministers.   But it is meant that
trash has been more than usually rampant
in recent years, and that it is habitually
viewed with a mischievous lenience and
toleration.   There is more than common
need of wholesome censure, as well of the
public taste as of the pernicious doctrine
that it is the province and policy of thinkers, writers, and managers to follow the
people instead of leading them.

II.

THE STORY OF MARY DUFF.

1794 — 1857.

MRS. DUFF, whose maiden name was Mary Dyke, was born in London in 1794, and died in New York in 1857. Her father was an Englishman, in the service of the East India Company, and he died abroad while she was a child. She was one of three sisters, all of whom adopted the profession of the stage, — making their first appearance in 1809 at a Dublin theatre, — and all of whom were remarkable for beauty of person and winning sweetness of character. She was early solicited in marriage by the poet Moore, who had acted with her in a benefit performance, and whose lyrics contain more than one allusion to that object of his love. He was thirty-one years old at that time. The offer was declined, and the poet subsequently wedded her sister, Elizabeth. Mary, meantime, had plighted her troth to John R. Duff, an actor of the

Dublin theatre, — an actor whom so good
a judge as William B. Wood, the famous
comedian and manager, accounted in after
years to be but little inferior to Elliston, —
and to him she was married in her sixteenth
year. They immediately came to America.
Mr. Duff's first appearance in this country
was made on November 2, 1810, at the Federal Street theatre, Boston, but his wife
did not appear till December 31, when she
came out as Juliet. Her public career
lasted from that time till 1838, when it
came to an end in New Orleans. She was
on the stage a little less than thirty years.
Her growth seems to have been slow; but
she bloomed into distinction and became
the most eminent and admired actress upon
the American stage. Boston was her
stronghold; but for five years, from 1812
to 1817, she was a member of the great
Philadelphia company of Warren and Wood,
and there, and on the New-York stage, she
likewise conquered an illustrious place. In
1828 she accompanied her husband to London, and acted at Drury Lane, as Isabella
— with Macready as Biron. Young, Cooper,
and Wallack were in the cast, and the Child
was played by Miss Lane, now Mrs. John
Drew, the consummate Mrs. Malaprop of

our time. Mr. and Mrs. Duff soon returned
to America, and never afterward left these
shores. In 1831 Mr. Duff died. He had
been for some time in poor health and he
had declined in professional popularity —
while his wife, at first viewed as his inferior
in ability, had surpassed and eclipsed him.
Yet, at his best, he was an actor whom
some writers of his day were inclined to
rank with the renowned George Frederick
Cooke. Mr. Ireland mentions two hundred
and ninety-two parts that were played by
him, — among which are Hamlet, Benedick,
The Stranger, Young Rapid, Doricourt, Me-
grim, Werter, and Robinson Crusoe. He
was one of the thorough old-school actors
who could play every line of dramatic business. His wife had the same sort of proficiency. She personified more than two
hundred and twenty characters — the list
still remaining incomplete. She was especially famous in Isabella, in *The Fatal
Marriage*, Jane Shore, Mrs. Haller, Mrs.
Beverley, Hermione, Statira, Belvidera,
Juliet, Portia, Tullia, Mary Stuart, and
Lady Macbeth. After her husband's death
Mrs. Duff had a hard struggle with poverty,
— as she was the mother of ten children,
and as acting, though of the best order, was

poorly paid in those days. In 1826, in New
York, Mr. and Mrs. Duff received jointly,
during ten weeks, a salary of only $55 a
week, together with the net proceeds of one
benefit. There is a contrast between the
days of Mrs. Duff and those of Jumbo.
Some of the "artists" who can obtain
great payments now are scarcely able to do
more than strum a banjo or whistle through
a jews'-harp. It was dramatic art that was
admired once ; it is often only entertain-
ment that is admired now.

About the year 1836 Mrs. Duff was married to Mr. J. G. Seaver, and there is no
record of her having been on the stage later
than May 30, 1838. She lived in New Orleans, renounced the stage, left the Catholic
faith, and became a Methodist ; and for
many years her life was devoted to works
of piety and benevolence. It appears that
she ultimately became unhappy in marriage. Her last years were passed in obscurity. Nobody knew either what had
become of Mary Duff, or where she lived,
or whether indeed she was alive, or where
she died, or where she was buried — till as
late as the year 1874. That she had disap-
peared from New Orleans, with Mr. Seaver,
in 1854, was the last ascertainable fact of

her history. They came privately to New York, and the once great and renowned actress, now a sad, subdued, broken-spirited old lady, took up her abode with her youngest daughter, Mrs. I. Reillieux, at No. 36 West Ninth street, where on September 5, 1857, she died. Her disease was cancer, and she was destroyed by internal hemorrhage. An article in *The Philadelphia Sunday Mercury*, August 9, 1874, written by Mr. James Rees, gives an account of the strange circumstances of her burial. According to that authority the remains of Mrs. Duff-Seaver were laid in the receiving tomb at Greenwood, September 6, 1857, and shortly afterward those of her daughter, Mrs. Reillieux, were likewise laid there; but on April 15, 1858, both those bodies were thence removed and were finally buried in the same grave, which is No. 805, in Lot 8999, in that part of the cemetery known as "The Hill of Graves" — the certificate describing them as "Mrs. Matilda I. Reillieux & Co." The grave was then marked with a headstone, inscribed with the words, "My Mother and Grandmother." There seems to have been a purpose to conceal the identity of Mrs. Seaver with Mrs. Duff, and to hide the fact

that the mother of Mrs. Reillieux had ever
been on the stage.   But the grave of the
great actress was finally discovered, and
many a pilgrim, honouring the memory of
genius and virtue, will pause beside it, with
reverence, as the years drift away.

The Life of Mary Duff has been written,
with laborious care and devoted zeal, by that
ripe and admirable dramatic antiquarian
and scholar, Joseph N. Ireland : and his
book is replete with interesting facts and
significant critical opinions.   The name of
that author, well and widely known by
his comprehensive *Records of the New-
York Stage*, is a guarantee of accuracy and
fulness of theatrical detail.   He knows the
history of our stage ; his judgment is sound,
his taste severe, his style simple.   In the
present instance he has chosen, instead of
writing an exclusively personal portrayal
and analysis of his heroine, to suggest her
greatness in the dramatic art, and to reproduce her identity, by reflecting the impression that she made upon the times
through which she lived.   Mr. Ireland frequently saw Mrs. Duff upon the stage, and
therefore he might have spoken altogether
from his own knowledge, without reference
to the opinions of other contemporaries.

But he has preferred to offer an unembel-
lished chronicle, and, with characteristic
reticence and modesty, to yield the prece-
dence to those old journals in which Mrs.
Duff's performances were first discussed,
at a time when they were as real to their
public as those of Ada Rehan and Ellen
Terry are to the public of to-day.

As it is half a century since Mrs. Duff
retired from the stage there cannot be
many persons extant who remember her
acting. Those who do will rejoice to see
it commemorated. Those who do not must
construct for themselves the best ideal that
their imagination can form out of the
testimony that her biographer's devotion
has collected. Mrs. Duff seems to have
been lovely more than beautiful ; strong in
the affectionate, melting charms of womanhood rather than the resolute, commanding, brilliant intellect ; a person fitted to
embody the heroines that entice and en-
thrall by their irresistible tenderness and
grace ; magical with the glamour of romance ; sacred in the majesty of grief ;
fascinating in tears ; and never so entirely
triumphant as when overwhelmed with
misery. The character of the parts in
which she was best certainly point at that

conclusion. Hermione — not Shakespeare's but the heroine of *The Distrest Mother*, taken from Racine's *Andromaque* — was a great success in her person. Jeannie Deans, Cordelia, Mrs. Haller and Mrs. Beverley were all perfect, as embodied by her. The dying scene of Tullia was one of her most tremendous and harrowing efforts. Her Lady Randolph was thought the best since Mrs. Siddons. Her madness in Belvidera was perfection. Those indications accord with the ideal of a soulful woman radiant with the essential spirit of her sex. She moved like a queen. The outline of her head and face was classic. She had dark, brilliant eyes, and she had a voice that swept from the clarion call of frantic passion to the softest accents of maternal love. The play of her countenance was incessant and wonderful ; and in purity and smoothness her elocution was perfect music. Such glorious creatures are seldom vouchsafed to earth. It is no wonder that they are worshipped. It is lamentable, beyond words, to think of the wretched fate that usually attends their steps and darkens round the ghastly tragedy of their closing hours.

III.

THE ELDER BOOTH.

1796 — 1852.

THE life of Junius Brutus Booth was full of incident, and yet, — aside from occurrences within his mind, on the theatre of his intellectual and spiritual experience, — it did not comprise many important events. He lived a few months more than fifty-six years. He was born in St. Pancras Parish, London, May 1, 1796, and he died on board of a steamboat, in the Mississippi river, November 30, 1852. His grandfather, John Booth, was a silversmith. His grandmother, Elizabeth Wilkes, was a relative of that able demagogue, Wilkes the Agitator. His father, Richard Booth, was a lawyer, and a Briton who, believing in "Wilkes and Liberty," also reverenced the character of Washington — a different man from the member for Middlesex. Junius was well educated, and he early showed a taste for literature and the arts. His first essays at the practical business of life were experimental. He tried printing; he tried the British navy; he tried painting and sculpture; and he tried the law; but all those trials came to nothing. At last he hit upon the right vocation and became an actor. That was in 1813 — and he remained on the stage from that time till the end of his days, a period of thirty-nine years; so that he had a professional career lasting four years longer than that of Garrick and ten years longer than that of Kean.

He began modestly, as Campillo, in Tobin's fine comedy of *The Honeymoon*, December 13, 1813, at Deptford, at a salary of one pound a week. Then for three years he led the life of a strolling player — a life which to a hardy youth of seventeen must have been a pleasant one, more especially as it involved a trip to the Continent. One of the first writers whose favourable opinion he attracted was the malignant Anthony Pasquin (Dr. Thomas Williams), who gave him advice, in a small way, characteristic of the man. Booth's first appearance in London was made in his novitiate, when he came forth, at Covent Garden, as Silvius, in *As You Like It*, and when Miss Sally Booth, who was one of the players there,

considerately suggested that he should add
e to his name, so that her name might not
be disgraced by implied association or relationship with him. After that he took to
the provinces again, and presently, at
Brighton, an accidental opportunity arrived
for him to win exceptional distinction. Edmund Kean had been announced there, to
play Sir Giles Overreach, but he did not
come, and Booth was assigned as a substitute for the famous actor — then in the prosperous morning of his enormous success.
It was a perilous ordeal, but the young
aspirant passed it with honour, and the
tide of his fortunes began to rise. On February 12, 1817, he was allowed a trial night
at Covent Garden, as Richard III., and he
acted there with such splendid ability that
the adherents of Kean, and even Kean himself, presently became alarmed at the apparition of so dangerous a rival.

Many pages have been written about the
troubles which thereupon ensued betwixt
Covent Garden and Drury Lane. It seems
certain that an effort was made, in which
Kean was an active participant, to lure
Booth away from the former theatre, to
engage him at the latter, to make him act
with Kean, at a disadvantage to himself,

and then finally to shelve him. To some
extent the scheme succeeded. Booth, never
a worldly-wise person, was only in his
twenty-first year at that time, and he fell
an easy prey to the wiles of his enemies.
He could not obtain the salary that he
wanted at Covent Garden; he was under
no contract; he was adroitly tempted by
Kean, who personally called on him; and
so he went to Drury Lane, and came out
there as Iago, to Kean's Othello, February
20, 1817; but, presently, as soon as he
ascertained the significance of Kean's sudden friendship, he made his peace with
Covent Garden and went back. A riot
followed, and Kean's friends, in the capacity of "wolves," distinguished themselves
by much belligerent vociferation, so that
Booth, for a time, was put to silence. But
all the uproar by and by subsided, and
Booth continued to act at Covent Garden,
and elsewhere in London. The most that
can be said, in just censure of his conduct
in that business, is that he acted with irres-
olution and the weakness of inexperience.
But he is not the only young man that ever
made a mistake; and the graver fault was
theirs who perplexed and misled him. His
subsequent career in Great Britain was

comprised within four years, in the course
of which time he appeared in Edinburgh,
Glasgow, Dublin, and other cities. In the
spring of 1820 he acted King Lear at Covent
Garden, with success, and in the summer
of the same year he appeared in a round of
plays, with Kean, at Drury Lane. On January 18, 1821, he was married to Miss Mary
Anne Holmes, and in company with his
wife, after a visit to France and to the
Island of Madeira, he came to America,
landing at Norfolk, Va., on June 30, that
year. The rest of his life was passed in
America, although he visited England, and
acted there, in 1825–27, and again in 1836.
A notable incident of the first of those
visits was his absolute reconciliation with
Kean: "He has been quite ill and looks
wretchedly," Booth wrote at that time ; "I
passed an hour with him, last night, at his
quarters, and reconciled our ancient mis-
understanding."

Booth's first appearance on the American
stage was made, July 6, 1821, at Richmond,
Virginia, as Richard III.; his last at the
St. Charles Theatre, New Orleans, November 19, 1852, as Sir Edward Mortimer and
John Lump. Between those extremes lies
the story of his American career. It was

one of brilliancy and waywardness, attended
by many stirring triumphs, darkened by
errors of human frailty, but rewarded with
a moderate competence of wealth, and
rounded by a noble professional fame.
The details of it are the details of numerous engagements in various cities. In New
York Booth was conspicuously associated
with the old Park Theatre, the Bowery, and
the National; in Boston, with the Tremont,
the Federal, and the Museum; in both
cities, and indeed throughout the United
States, he was a prodigious favourite. He
never remained long in one place and he
seldom assumed business responsibilities.
He was once stage-manager for Henry Wallack, at the Chatham Garden, in New York,
and once stage-manager for Caldwell, at
the Camp, in New Orleans, and he leased
and managed for a while the Adelphi, in
Baltimore. In England he had acted with
Kean; in America he acted with Cooper
and Forrest; and in certain directions he
surpassed them all. At New Orleans, in
1828, he acted Orestes, in the French language and with a French company, and
he did that with such brilliancy and such
tremendous force of passion that he was
hailed, by a French audience, as another
Talma.

Almost immediately after Booth's arrival
in America he bought a farm at Belair,
Harford County, Maryland, in a wooded,
romantic solitude, far from the abodes of
men, and that hermitage he made his head-
quarters, emerging, from time to time, to
dazzle and astonish mankind upon the
stage, and straightway escaping again into
his retreat. On that domain he forbade the
use of animal food, and he would permit no
living creature — not even a reptile — to be
killed. Ten children were born to him, of
whom Edwin was the seventh. He loved
his children with a passionate devotion; but
his mode of rearing them was as eccentric
as his management of his own wonderful
faculties. He wished them to till the ground
and to learn mechanical trades, and he
counted education, such as he had himself
received, superfluous and useless. He loved
to work in the earth, to watch growing
plants, to have the companionship of trees,
and to listen to the sounds of the forest.
At certain periods, and especially after
death had bereaved him of two of his children, under pitiful circumstances, he was the
victim of dark moods, in which his reason
became unsettled, and in which his actions
were strange and fantastic, weird or comi-

cal, or absolutely and palpably insane.
Many stories are told of his vagrant wanderings in the woods ; his long walks from
city to city ; his midnight rides in the dress
of Richard or Hamlet ; his capricious treatment of audiences ; his funeral ceremonials
over dead animals and birds ; his compas-
sionate sympathy with vagabonds ; his mysterious disappearances ; his moody reveries ;
his inequality as an actor ; his fitful industry ; his strange fluctuations between a cos-
mopolitan fellowship with mankind and a
Timon-like isolation ; his power to read even
the Lord's Prayer in such a way as to con-
vulse his hearers with pathetic emotion ; and
his terrific outbursts of ferocious passion
upon the stage, which made his associates
tremble for their lives. Once, after playing
Cassius perfectly during the first three acts,
he suddenly entered, for the fourth, walk-
ing airily on the tips of his toes. Once he
went through the whole performance of
Pierre in a whisper, only raising his voice
at the last to remark, with placid satisfaction, "We have deceived the Senate." On
still another occasion he felt it necessary to
scrape the ham out of some sandwiches
that had been provided for his repast,
just before he went on to act Shylock.

There is no end to illustrative incidents of that kind. The reminiscences of old actors and play-goers have preserved scores of such traits, and among them, no doubt, many fictions. Booth was a wild, strange being, as mysterious and as grand as "The Ancient Mariner," which of all poems he loved best, and which is an apt emblem of his haunted spirit.

Booth's detractors — and, of course, he had them — did not hesitate to accuse him of simulating eccentricity. One of the old theatrical writers says it, in so many words. No sillier calumny was ever uttered. The honesty of his life, the agony of his sufferings, and the revelation that he made, in his acting, of the depths of human misery, answer and dispose of it forever. No enemy ever ventured to impute to him, living or dead, a dishonourable action. He promoted no public scandal. He brought no disgrace upon his profession. He had no professional animosities. He persecuted nobody. He was just and kind in the relations of domestic and social life. He wore the laurels of a unique and unparalleled fame with more than the modesty and simplicity of a child. The public loved him, and when he died the news brought tears

to the eyes of thousands. Rufus Choate,
himself a great genius and most competent
to understand such a nature, spoke the general feeling of that hour, when he exclaimed,
" There are no more actors."

The fact which seems to suggest the elder
Booth, if not to define him, as an actor, is
that he was heedless and imperfect as an
artist, but electrical and fascinating as a
man. He would, for example, when acting
Macbeth, deliberately go to the wing and
get a broadsword with which to fight the
final battle, and would do that in full view
of the audience — just as Ristori, when acting Lady Macbeth, would carry her husband's letter to the side and throw it away.
He did not care, when acting Richard,
whether he wore an old dressing-gown or
a royal robe, and he heeded little where
other persons entered or stood, so that they
got on and were somewhere. His acting
had no touch of the finish of Macready.
But the soul that he poured into it was
awful and terrible : the face, the hands, the
posture, the movement, all was incarnate
eloquence ; and when the lightning of the
blue-gray eyes flashed, and the magnificent
voice gave out its deep thunder-roll, or
pealed forth its sonorous trumpet-notes, the

hearts of his hearers were swept away as on the wings of a tempest. Each tone and each action was then absolutely right. Even his marvellous elocution, which brought out the subtle meaning of every sound in every syllable, seemed inspired, — such and so great was the vitality which a glorious imagination, thoroughly aroused, could strike out of a deep and passionate heart. He played many parts: there is descriptive record of him in about twenty of the greatest: but probably he was at his best in Richard III., Sir Giles Overreach,[1] Sir Edward Mortimer, Iago, and Shylock. Edmund Kean excelled in depicting misery and awakening passion. To him belonged such parts as Othello and the Stranger. Booth's peculiar grandeur was in the region of the supernatural and the terrible.

[1] An informing remark upon the elder Booth was made to me by Joseph Jefferson, who had often acted with him: "The greatest tragic actor I have ever seen was Junius Booth. He was not the equal of Macready as an intellectual artist, but his spirit was extraordinary and overwhelming. When he acted Sir Giles you never thought of looking at his gestures and motions; it was what was inside of the man that you saw. His face, in the last act, used to twitch: he was like a caged wild beast."

IV.

FALSTAFF HACKETT.

THE dramatic veteran James Henry
Hackett died on December 28, 1871,
at Jamaica, Long Island, in the seventy-
second year of his age. He departed in the
ripeness of time and the maturity of experience, with all his honours gathered and
all the purposes and possibilities of his
career fulfilled. His death, therefore, was
one of those bereavements to which the
mind submits — with deep sorrow, indeed
— but with natural resignation. Nothing
of that consternation, nothing of that bitterness of grief, with which we contemplate a life that seems prematurely broken,
could mingle with regret for the loss of that
admirable artist and original and interesting character. He had finished his work.
He had enjoyed, in liberal abundance, the
rewards of success and the laurels and
privileges of well-earned fame. Nothing
was left for him but rest, and into that he
entered. "Momus himself is dead."

The record of Hackett's life has been written by his own hand — in an *Autobiography* which has enjoyed a wide circulation among the readers of theatrical literature. He was born in New York, at No. 72 William Street, on March 15, 1800. His father was a Hollander and had been a lieutenant in the Life Guards of the Prince of Orange. His mother was the daughter of the Rev. Abraham Keteltas, of Jamaica, Long Island — a clergyman of ability and learning, of whom it is said that in the discharge of his ministerial duties he often officiated in three different languages. From those sources it was natural that the boy should inherit great sturdiness of physical constitution and a strong impulse towards intellectual pursuits. While he was yet a child his parents removed to Jamaica, where, in 1805, he became a pupil at the Union Hall Academy — then directed by Mr. Eigenbrogdt, a teacher of local repute. He remained there ten years. In 1815 he entered Columbia College, where, however, he studied but one year. In 1817 he was a law student with Gen. Robert Bogardus; and it is intimated that at this time he first dabbled in theatrical pursuits. In 1818 he engaged his services as a clerk. In 1819

he married Miss Catherine Leesugg, a singing actress at the Park Theatre, whom he
withdrew from the stage. From 1820 to
1826 he remained in mercantile pursuits,
living part of the time in Utica and part of
the time in New York. Unsuccessful spec-
ulations, during 1825, led to bankruptcy,
and he thereupon reverted to his early taste
for the drama. His wife reappeared, on
February 27, 1826, at the Park Theatre, as
the Countess, in *The Devil's Bridge*, and
as Marian Ramsay.

On March 1, 1826, Hackett made his
first appearance at the same house, and in
the character of Justice Woodcock. The
effort was a failure. On March 10, however,
he made a second endeavour, enacting Sylvester Daggerwood, and introducing imita-
tions of Mathews, Kean, and other actors.
Those were remarkably clever, and they at
once drew attention to the actor, who thereupon determined to persevere in the newly-
chosen calling. His third appearance, on
June 19, was made in the Yankee character of Uncle Ben, and the French character of Morbleau, in *Monsieur Tonson*.
Success continued to attend him. His
Dromio, first seen on October 25, 1826,
made an emphatic hit. Towards the end

of that year he went to England, making
his first professional appearance in London, at Covent Garden, April 6, 1827. A
little later he acted at the Surrey theatre,
and gave a clever imitation of Edmund
Kean's Richard III. It is a notable fact
that, although Hackett's best achievements
and most conspicuous triumphs were won
in comedy, his aspirations were almost invariably directed towards tragedy. Upon
his return to America he appeared in several new parts, one of which was Rip Van
Winkle — in which, for many years, he
held preëminence in public favor. His
personation of that character was based
directly upon Irving's sketch, and it was
a true and marvellously strong reproduction
of the commonplace, good-natured vaga-
bond, whom, in our time, the delicate genius
of Jefferson has — by the skilful alteration
of circumstances, the infusion of a subtle
spirit of poetry, and a perfect method —
lifted into the higher realm of the ideal
and made a poem as well as a fact.
Hackett's acting, at the point where Rip
Van Winkle hears that his wife is dead,
gave as true a touch of nature as ever was
seen. Facial expression, voice, and gesture
— the mournful, half physical reminiscence,

the convulsive sob, the artless, involuntary
utterance — all concurred to reveal the deep
sincerity of that love which was the man's
second nature, and which dignified his
wretchedness, his rags, and his degradation.
That, and certain bits of his Monsieur Mal-
let and his Falstaff, displayed Hackett for
what he really was — an original, natural,
unique actor in parts of serio-comic character. The public fully accepted him as an
artist of that class ; and it was not till new
lights had arisen in a newer time, and the
powers of the veteran began to wane beneath the chill of frosty age, that his grip
upon popularity was relaxed.

In 1829 and 1830 he was, for a time, associated with the management of the Bowery
and the Chatham Theatres. It was about
this time that he first played Falstaff. In
1832 he made a second visit to England,
and in 1840, 1845, and 1851 he made other
visits to that country, and successful professional tours. In 1837 he managed the
National Theatre in New York ; and in
1849 he was lessee and manager of the
Astor-Place Opera House, when certain
ruffians, adherents of Forrest, attempted to
drive Macready from the stage and thus
caused a disastrous and fatal riot. In

1854 Hackett introduced Grisi and Mario to the American public, presenting them in New York, at Castle Garden, on September 4, in that year. Subsequently, on October 2, the New York Academy of Music was, for the first time, opened to the public, and those artists appeared there, under Hackett's direction. The professional career of the actor during the last seventeen years of his life was marked by no considerable vicissitude. He continued to act — in an itinerant and somewhat fitful and obscure manner — till the season of 1867–68, when he abandoned active employment. His first wife died in 1840. They had three sons, of whom the second, John K. Hackett, became well known upon the Bench. Hackett contracted a second marriage in 1866 and his widow and a child of two years survived him. The sickness that carried him off was the first serious ailment that he ever suffered. His disease was dropsy, complicated by a disorder of the lungs.

Hackett, as an actor, was remarkable chiefly for his Falstaff. That was last seen in New York when the veteran played his last engagement at Booth's Theatre, from November 29 to December 25, 1869. He

acted in both *Henry the Fourth* and *The
Merry Wives of Windsor*. His Falstaff was
a symmetrical blending of intellect and
sensuality. The external attributes were
perfect. The burly form, the round, ruddy
face, the rimy fringe of gray whiskers, the
bright, penetrating, merry eyes, the rows
of even, white teeth, the strong, hard voice,
the pompous, gross, selfish, animal demeanour, tempered at times by wily sagacity and
by the perfect manner of an old man-of-the-
world, combined to make that an admirably
distinct and natural embodiment in all that
relates to form. As to the spirit of the
work there were wide differences of critical
opinion — as is always the case with reference to art of decided character and
conspicuous merit. It is only concerning
things of no importance that, as a rule,
everybody is agreed. The humour of
Hackett's Falstaff was not so much unctuous as it was satirical. He interpreted a
mind that was merry, but one in which
merriment was strongly tinctured with
scorn. It knew nothing about virtue, except that some people trade on that attribute ; and it knew nothing about sweetness,
except that it is a property of sugar and
a good thing in "sack." The essence of

his conception was most perceptible in two scenes — in the delivery of the soliloquy on Honour, in *Henry IV.*, and in the fat knight's scene, at first alone, then with Bardolph, and then with Master Brook, after the ducking in the Thames, in *The Merry Wives of Windsor*. The first — in its sly shrewdness, contempt for self-sacrifice, and utter inability to comprehend nobleness of motive or conduct — was almost sardonic. The latter — in its embodiment of the discomfort of a balked and fretted sensualist, and the rage and self-scorn of a sensible man at having been physically humiliated — was indescribably ludicrous, because of its absolute and profound seriousness. Those indications pointed to a stern individuality, latent within the humour and the boisterous conviviality of the man — and that was the basis of Hackett's ideal. With respect to method he was a bold artist. He painted with broad and vigorous strokes and gave little heed to details and delicacy of finish. His Sir Pertinax MacSycophant and his O'Callaghan, however, were drawn and coloured with extraordinary care and taste, and those showed him — at least in the latter part of his career — to be a master of the art of elaboration. He played Lear and Hamlet, in 1840, for the first time, and very seldom thereafter; but he made no impression with those tragic parts. He possessed gravity but not solemnity. He knew the passions by sight, but not by feeling. His greatness consisted in the vigorous illustration of strongly defined, eccentric characters, and in the unconscious expression of that everlasting comicality which such characters dispense upon the conduct of life.

Hackett held his profession in sincere esteem and strove by all the means at his command to advance its interest and its repute. To him is due the honour of projecting the plan for a Shakespeare Monument in the Central Park, the corner-stone of which was laid, under his auspices, on April 23, 1864 — the Shakespeare Tercentenary. Hackett was highly respected as a gentleman and prized as a friend. His life was passed in the conscientious service of art and it was crowned with the laurels of integrity and honour.

V.

A SHORT LIFE OF FORREST.

1806 — 1872.

ON the night of November 22, 1872, while listening, in Steinway Hall, to Edwin Forrest's reading of the tragedy of *Othello*, a presentiment that he would soon and suddenly die was borne in upon my thoughts with such affecting force and solemnity that I was impelled to choose what words from his lips should be the last ever heard by me, and, obeying that impulse, I left the hall immediately upon his conclusion of the heart-broken utterance of desolate agony which ends with "Othello's occupation's gone." He spoke that speech with more than a mournful beauty of intonation. He spoke it from his inmost soul — pouring out in those few words an agonizing sense of utter failure, forlorn wretchedness, and irremediable woe. The memory of that relentless trouble and hopeless sorrow was still

fresh, when the announcement came that
Forrest was dead. He expired on December 12, 1872, at his home in Philadelphia,
in the sixty-seventh year of his age.

A great vitality, an enormous individuality of character, a boundless ambition, a
tempestuous spirit, a life of rude warfare
and often of harsh injustice, an embittered
mind, and an age laden with disappointment and pain were thus ended. Forrest
— partly from natural bias to the wrong
and partly from the force of circumstances
and the inexorable action of time — had
made shipwreck of his happiness ; had cast
away many golden opportunities ; had outlived his fame ; had outlived many of his
friends and alienated others ; had seen the
fabric of his popularity begin to crumble ;
had seen the growth of new tastes and the
rise of new idols ; had found his claims as
an actor, if accepted by many among the
multitude, rejected by many among the
judicious ; and, in wintry age, broken in
health, dejected in spirit, and thwarted in
ambition, had come to the "last scene of
all," with great wealth, indeed, but with
little of peace or hope. His nature — which
should have been noble, for it contained
elements of greatness and beauty — was dis-

eased with arrogance, passion, and cruelty. It warred with itself and it made him desolate. He had long been a wreck. There was nothing before him here but an arid waste of suffering; and, understanding him thus, it was a relief to think of him beyond the reach of trouble, and where neither care, sorrow, unreasoning passion, resentment against the world, nor physical pain could torment him any more.

The life of Edwin Forrest was unusually crowded with such incidents as naturally attend the career of a popular actor, and also with such incidents as are but too apt to attend the development of a rudely energetic character, struggling, — from worldly motives and by worldly ways, — out of the obscurity of poverty into the distinction of riches. In his bright days he was the conspicuous figure in many popular pageants, and he was also the originator of many quarrels and the centre of much strife. He filled a large space in the history of the American stage. His name and his personal presence were familiar to the people in many cities. He was the founder of a distinct school of acting and there were elements in his rugged and turbulent individuality which made it interesting, significant, and usefully responsive to intelligent study.

Edwin Forrest was born in Philadelphia on March 9, 1806. His father was a native of Scotland; his mother a native of Germany. His father was a commercial traveller, in which vocation he came to America. In boyhood Edwin's health was delicate, and until he reached the age of fourteen, when he began to get strong, his relatives doubted whether he would survive to man's estate. At about the age of fourteen he went into the West, and from that change of residence he derived great benefit; his constitution turned out to be hardy, and eventually he became one of the most athletic men of his generation. As a child he exhibited taste and aptitude for declamation. At the age of eleven he participated in a theatrical representation — being then a member of a private amateur dramatic club in Philadelphia. Once, in a performance given by that club, he played Harlequin, wearing nankeen trousers which he had himself marked in squares and painted. Another time he acted a female part, and, on being hissed by a young person in the audience whom he recognised, he came to the footlights, and addressed the sibilant spectator in these words: "D—n you, D——, you wait till I get through with this part, and I'll lick you like h—l." The incident is significant. To "lick like h—l" everybody who presumed to disapprove of either his acting, his conduct, or his character, was, during many years, the spontaneous and intense desire of Forrest; for he thought that the disapproval was always fictitious and hostile, and that the "licking," accordingly, would be a just and suitable resentment. His first appearance on the regular stage was made at the Walnut-street theatre, Philadelphia, on November 27, 1820, when he acted Douglas, in Home's play of that name,— an ambitious attempt to be made by a boy of fourteen. It attracted little attention, but it seems to have shown precocity, both physical and mental. His next part, played in the same engagement, was Frederick, in *Lover's Vows* — the play that Mrs. Inchbald made out of Kotzebue's drama of the *Natural Son*. That production, shelved for many years, used to be popular, and Frederick was a favourite part with beginners on the stage. Still later, for his benefit, the young actor appeared as Octavian, in Colman's play — on

episodes in *Don Quixote* — of *The Moun-
taineers;* and this closed the first chapter
of his professional record.

Then came the removal into the West.
Forrest went thither under engagement
to Messrs. Collins and Jones, actors and
managers well-known in their day on the
southwestern theatrical circuit. They were
then managing the Cincinnati theatre; and
it was there, in the early part of 1822, that
Forrest made his first appearance under
their direction. The part that he acted was
young Melfort, in Andrew Cherry's now
disused comedy of *The Soldier's Daughter;*
and subsequently, for his benefit, he made
his first attempt at *Richard III.* Mention
of those performances occurs in the Autobiography of Sol Smith, who was then
editing a paper in Cincinnati. "When I
gave a very favourable opinion of Forrest's
acting, in the comparatively trifling character of Melfort," says that writer, "my
brother editors laughed at me; and afterwards, when he played Richard for his
benefit, and I prophesied his greatness,
they set me down as little less than a
madman. 'He was a clever boy, certainly,'
they said, 'but puffing would ruin him.'"
The stock company of which Forrest was

a member comprised, besides Messrs. Collins and Jones and himself, Messrs. Scott, Davis, Eberle, Henderson, and Groshon; Mrs. Pelby, Mrs. Riddle, Miss Riddle, Miss Eliza Riddle, then a child, and Miss Fenton. In the summer of 1822 they went to Louisville; but business proved bad and a party of them, including Forrest, presently returned to Cincinnati, and appeared at the Globe theatre. It was there that he first acted Othello. It was there also that he acted what had never before been presented on any stage, an American negro. That was in a local farce, written by Sol Smith, called *The Tailor in Distress*. It must have been during this engagement, also, that he first played Corinthian Tom, in *Tom and Jerry*, of which part he was the original representative in America.

Enterprise in the Globe theatre, however, did not thrive, and that enterprise was soon relinquished. Forrest, accompanied by the Riddle family and some other players, then made a trip from Cincinnati, performing as occasion served or could be made in the small towns of Ohio. That was a time of hardship and trial to the adventurous young actor, and first and last he fell into straits of misfortune. Once, near

the town of Dayton, he applied to a farmer
for employment and was set at work saw-
ing wood, by which means he earned something to eat and a little money for travelling
expenses. Once he assumed the character
of an itinerant preacher, and having delivered a sermon, in the alleged interest of a
missionary cause, "took up a collection,"
from his "hearers," and so relieved his
pressing necessity. On one occasion he
travelled, with his party of players, twenty-
two miles on foot — frcm Lebanon to Cincinnati, and then across the Ohio to Newport — where the tired Thespians acted
Douglas and *Miss in her Teens*, to an
auditory that had paid only one dollar at
the door. All this while Forrest was en-
during the rough weather of hard fortune
and the preliminary drudgery, without
which, in some form, there is no success
in the actor's art. In the autumn of 1822
Forrest and his companions joined their
old managers, Messrs. Collins and Jones,
at Lexington, Ky., but those persons presently relinquished theatrical business, and
Forrest then engaged himself to James
H. Caldwell of the American theatre,
New Orleans. Sol Smith says that the
young actor proposed to break this New

Orleans engagement and stay with him at Lexington ; and that, because this rash and indiscreet proposal was declined, he went off in a pet, and procured employment in a circus at a salary of twelve dollars a week. " By dint of hard lecturing and strong argument," adds Smith, " I finally prevailed on him to abandon his new profession." Forrest's first appearance in New Orleans, February 4, 1823, was made as Jaffier, in *Venice Preserved*, and he remained in that city and its neighbourhood for about two years. His way of life while he was there appears to have been somewhat loose and violent. He was less remarkable as an actor than as a reveller. When he came again to the North he drifted into Albany, where he got an engagement at the Albany theatre, under the management of Charles Gilfert, who paid to him $7.50 a week. It was during this engagement that he was fortunate enough to attract the notice and approbation of Edmund Kean, to whom he played second parts. It was during this engagement, also, that he made his second appearance in his native city. That was at the Walnut-street theatre, where, for the benefit of C. S. Porter, he acted Jaffier.

Three nights later he acted Rolla. Both those personations were much admired. Then came his first emphatic hit in New York. A friend of his — Woodhull of the Park theatre — was to have a benefit, and Forrest was fortunate enough to get an opportunity to act for it. The part that he chose for this first appearance at the leading theatre in the country was Othello. It was deemed an audacious presumption. Gilfert, fearing the worst of failure, strongly counselled him against the undertaking, and even went so far as to say that in case of an ensuing fiasco the actor would be discharged. Forrest, however, was not to be dissuaded nor intimidated. On May 23, 1826, the performance, accordingly, took place. The house was full, and when the curtain dropped upon the third act of the tragedy the new actor had won the first great success of his life.

The tide of favour now began to rise. Simpson immediately offered him an engagement on excellent terms at the Park; but Gilfert, who had just taken the Bowery theatre, of which he was the first lessee, succeeded in securing him for that theatre, for a salary of eight hundred dollars a year. The Bowery, under Gilfert's management, was the scene of great triumphs for Forrest. Among the parts which he there represented with extraordinary popular success were Damon, Jaffier, William Tell, and Marc Antony. He remained there nearly three years; but at the death of Gilfert, in 1829, he accepted an engagement at the Park. It began October 17, in that year, when he appeared as Damon. At that theatre Forrest long enjoyed a high popularity. It was there that he first acted Metamora and Spartacus, in John H. Stone's tragedy of *Metamora* (produced December 15, 1829), and Robert M. Bird's tragedy of *The Gladiator* (produced September 26, 1831), both of which plays were written with a special view to fit his talents and peculiarities, and in both of which his acting was the perfection of physical realism.

Time passed, and the tragedian grew more and more in the cordial estimation of hosts of New York admirers. In the summer of 1834 a company of citizens tendered to him the formal courtesy of a public banquet, and presented him with a gold medal in token of their homage. This medal, designed by the artist Ingham and engraved by C. C. Durand, bore on one side a portrait of the actor, inscribed with the words, *Histrioni optimo Edwino Forrest, viro præstanti;* and on the other a figure, emblematic of tragedy, with the words from Shakespeare. "Great in mouths of wisest censure." Forrest was now in the prime of manhood and the first flush of popularity, a person remarkable for muscular beauty, a voice of prodigious volume and melodious sweetness, and an intensely forcible style of depicting the emotional experience of turbulent characters. He had, within a brief time, acquired an extraordinary vogue and distinction. The local stage, not then able to exult in much tragic talent distinctively American, proudly claimed for this American actor an equal rank with the best foreign representatives of tragedy. The local newspapers teemed with his praise. All the favouring gales of fortune, indeed, concurred to blow in one direction, and thus far the young actor sailed before the wind. When, therefore, Forrest went to England — which he did at that time — it was natural that he should attract attention as a typical American actor. His reception was such as might well have touched the heart and flattered the intellectual pride of an ambitious and sensitive man.

Forrest made a trip through France, Italy, and Germany before entering England; but on October 17, 1836, at Drury Lane, he appeared as Spartacus in *The Gladiator*. That performance stirred the theatrical public with a sensation different from any it had known before, since it offered an unprecedented union of enormous physical vigour with uncommon talent for tragic acting. Great popularity ensued, and Forrest became a lion of the hour. It is worthy of mention that he received, at that time, especially kind treatment at the hands of Macready and from other persons eminent in the profession of the stage. Many and pleasant tokens of courtesy were also extended to him by members of the literary craft. Talfourd presided at a dinner which the Garrick Club tendered to the American actor, and Charles Kemble and Stephen Price gave to him swords which had once been the property, respectively, of John Kemble, Edmund Kean, and Talma. That period was, probably, the happiest in Forrest's life — though, had his nature been gentle, his ambition noble, and his conduct pure, it would have been, there is good reason to think, only the joyful dawn of a long day of ever-increasing happiness.

An event now occurred which was destined to shape and colour all the rest of his career. This was his meeting with Miss Catherine Norton Sinclair, daughter of the vocalist, John Sinclair, whom he wooed and won, and to whom he was married on June 23, 1837. The meeting and the marriage had been predicted before Forrest left America. There was every reason to suppose that the union would prove a happy one; but, twelve years later, it ended in a separation, in misery to both parties, in a bitter strife between their friends and adherents, and in distressful counter-suits at law betwixt husband and wife which were the fruitful source of scandal. The course pursued by Forrest, in a portion of his married life, is said to have been a course of cruelty and licentiousness. The line of conduct that he followed in the matter of the divorce was, to an astonishing degree, ignoble, ruthless, and wicked. It is not an exaggeration to say that it alienated from him, at once and forever, the sympathy of the better classes of the people. His wife was victorious in that contest. She procured her divorce from him, forfeiting none of her honours and legal rights; and, surviving many wrongs and much suffering, she lived to cast the flower of pity and pardon on his grave. [She died in New York, in 1891, and her grave is in the Silver Mount Cemetery in Staten Island.]

Immediately after their marriage Forrest and his wife came to America. The actor made his professional reappearance at Philadelphia, and was welcomed with enthusiasm. A public banquet, given in his honour in that city, at which Hon. J. R. Ingersoll presided, emphasised this greeting and indicated the pride and pleasure with which his prosperity and fame were generally recognised. From Philadelphia, still pursuing his triumph, Forrest proceeded to New York and appeared at the Park theatre. The receipts at the box-office on the first three nights of that engagement amounted to $4200. One of the especially important incidents of his career, at this period, was the production of *Jack Cade*, in which he played Aylmere — one of his most original and characteristic personations. This tragic drama was written for him by Robert T. Conrad of Philadelphia, and it was first acted on May 24, 1841, at the Park theatre.

Forrest's second visit to London was made in 1845. His wife went with him, and they moved at that time in circles of the intellectual and polished society of that metropolis, and also of the Scottish capital, which they presently visited. Forrest acted at the Princess's theatre, London. Here Sheridan Knowles — so great was his satisfaction with Forrest's Virginius — played, by his own offer, the part of Dentatus, on the occasion of the tragedian's benefit. Here, also, it happened that the public hissed Forrest's performance of Macbeth — one of the most ludicrous personations that ever mistaken sincerity submitted as a serious effort in tragedy. The annoyance which befell Forrest, in this instance, he chose to attribute, without reason or justification, to the hostile machinations of Macready ; and thereupon his conduct was what might have been expected from a man overfreighted with selfishness, conceit, and an explosive temper, and deficient in dignity of character. Happening to be in Edinburgh shortly afterwards, where Macready was acting, he went to the theatre to see the English tragedian as Hamlet, stood up conspicuously in a private box, and hissed at him. This proceeding, childishly petulant even if there had been a good reason for it, naturally inspired disgust for the American actor. Forrest strove to justify himself by a letter to the London *Times*, which, as first written, the editor of that journal declined to print — objecting to some abuse it contained of the respectable Edinburgh journal, *The Scotsman*. Ultimately, however, Forrest having amended his epistle so as to restrict it to the statement of his grievance, the London *Times* published the composition. The sequel is known. Out of this vain and silly resentment for an imaginary wrong grew, in later days, the shocking and disgraceful Astor-place riot and massacre in New York. Macready came to America in the season of 1848–49, making his third and last visit to this country, and acted at the Astor-place opera house, then managed by Niblo and James H. Hackett. The riot occurred on May 10, 1849. Macready acted Macbeth. A successful attempt to prevent him from finishing a performance of this part had been made, by riotous adherents of Forrest, on the night of the 8th ; but it was determined, by the respectable part of the play-going public, that Macready should have a chance to act unmolested the character of Macbeth, and hence the piece was immediately announced for repetition. Forrest was fulfilling a contemporary engagement at the Broadway theatre, from which place — as there is reason to believe, though perhaps the statement may not, at this late day, be susceptible of positive proof — he promoted the outbreak of brutal rowdyism which ensued, and which ended in the killing of twenty-two men, and the wounding of thirty-six others. Hard upon the heels of that riot came the domestic trouble between Forrest and his wife. The case went into the courts in 1850, and after the widest publicity of discussion and a liberal allowance of the law's delay, it resulted in the lady's complete justification.

On January 9, 1852, Forrest — riding on the storm — appeared at the Broadway theatre, and acted for sixty-nine successive nights, beginning and ending with Damon. After that time the story of his life concerns itself with a long series of professional engagements in different cities of the Union; with the piling up of immense wealth; with the eliciting of extravagant praises and of equally extreme vituperation; with his castle of Fonthill on the banks of the Hudson, his palace in Philadelphia, his theatrical library, his reclusive habits of living, his misanthropy, his frequent illness, and his gradual decline out of active professional labour and the fashion of the passing age. His last engagement in New York began on February 6, 1871, and continued three weeks. He appeared at the Fourteenth-street theatre as Lear and as Richelieu. A sudden illness afflicted him and he was compelled abruptly to desist. His final appearances occurred on the 19 and 22 of November, 1872, when at Steinway Hall, New York, he read from *Hamlet* and *Othello*.

Forrest was remarkable for his iron repose, his perfect precision of method, his immense physical force, his capacity for leonine banter, his fiery ferocity, and his occasional felicity of elocution in passages of monotone and colloquy. Strength and definiteness are always comprehensible and generally admirable. Forrest was the union of both. He resembled, in this, a rugged old tower, conspicuous in a landscape. The architecture may not be admired, but the building is distinctly seen and known. You might not like the actor, but you could not help seeing that he was the bold representative of a certain set of ideas in art. But while Forrest illustrated the value of earnestness and of assured skill, he also illustrated the law of classification in art as well as in humanity. All mankind — artists among the rest — are distinctly classified. We are what we are. Each man develops along his own grade, but never rises into a higher one. Hence the world's continual wrangling over representative men — wrangling between persons of different classes, who can never possibly become of one mind. Forrest was continually the theme of that sort of controversy. He represented the physical element in art. He was a landmark on the border line between physical and spiritual power. Natures kindred with his own admired him, followed him, reverenced him, as the finest type of artist. That was natural and inevitable. But there is another sort of nature — with which neither Forrest nor his admirers could sympathise — that asks continually for some great spiritual hero and leader ; that has crowned and uncrowned many false monarchs ; and that must forever hopelessly pursue its ideal. This nature feels what Shelley felt when he wrote of " the desire of the moth for the star." To persons of this order — and they are sufficiently numerous to constitute a large minority — Forrest's peculiar interpretations of character and passion were unsatisfactory. They admired his certainty of touch, his profound assurance, his solid symmetry. But they felt that something was wanting to complete the artist. They did not belong to his audience, and they were as much out of place in listening to him as a congregation of ultra Methodists would have been, listening to Emerson. He had nothing to say to them. He was great in his way, they perceived; but, like the Gallic wit, they also perceived that his way was small. To his natural admirers, on the contrary, he was great in his way, and his way was the greatest of ways. Those two parties long assailed and defended him. Fruitlessly, — for this kind of dispute cannot in nature come to an end or even to a compromise.

It has often been said of Forrest that he was a melodramatic actor. He was not; he was a tragedian. His Othello, his Virginius, and, in later years, his Lear were the sufficient proof of this. He had imagination, — though it was seldom informed by fine intelligence and never by spirituality, — and he had passion and tenderness. Even in Spartacus, though the method was melodramatic, there was a noble assumption of tender and manly attributes, which dwarfed the physical ebullitions. That which marred his acting, to the judicious, was that which marred his character. He was utterly selfish. He did not love dramatic art for its own sake, but because it was tributary to himself. The motives of his conduct were vanity, pride, self-assertion, and avarice of power, praise, and wealth. Aided by great physical strength, manly beauty, and natural talent, they impelled him — over many obstacles and much hardship — to prosperity and precarious eminence. But they did not conduct him to real greatness. His nature fulfilled itself, and for that reason his life was a failure. It was this which made him a pathetic object. He was never able, as a matter of destiny, to reach the goal which, nevertheless, he vaguely saw. To a man of imaginative temperament, picturesque attributes, and a heart susceptible of suffering, this was a sad fate. It resulted, not by reason of what he did, but by reason of what he was — a vast animal, bewildered by a grain of genius.

It is to the credit of Forrest that he remembered his early friend and manager,

William Jones, as a benefactor, and manifested toward him, in after years, a practical and commendable gratitude, giving him
shelter and bounty when these were greatly needed. Those early days of adventure
in the West and South were full of hardship for Forrest, and he appreciated keenly
and remembered long whatever kindness
was then extended to him — a stranger and
a struggling novice. It was in Forrest's
house in New York, in 1841, that Jones
suffered his last sickness and passed away.
Another man to whom Forrest was kind
was John Augustus Stone, over whose
grave in Philadelphia (where he died, a
suicide, June 1, 1834) stands a monument
inscribed with these words: "In Memory
of the Author of 'Metamora'; By His
Friend E. Forrest." The actor's best friend
was William Leggett, whose death, not
very long after they became attached com-
rades, bereaved him of a wise adviser, an
appreciative admirer, an intellectual prop,
a frank and fearless censor, and a companion whose influence was always for his
good.

Edwin Forrest was not a man whom it
is desirable to canonise. The tone of his
thoughts was coloured and the action of his

mind was controlled, during the best part of his career, by animal excitement, and that excitement was curbed by no intellectual prudence. So wholly did he believe in himself and so entirely did he find the rude mob in sympathy with him that until the shadows began to gather over his pathway he never conceived the idea that he might ever be in the wrong. If he ever imagined a state of things that he could deem to be properly adjusted, Edwin Forrest was its centre. In youth and early manhood he was boisterous, sensual, revengeful, and profligate. In age he was misanthropical. He was capable of good impulses and kind actions; but the impulses were often checked by distrust, and the actions were often prompted and molded by selfish aims. His vanity was prodigious. He thought himself the greatest of actors and of men. The least expression of dissent from his opinion, or of disapproval of what he had said or done, would sting him into an outburst of fury or madden him to a long fit of sullen resentment. The idea that under any conceivable circumstances his powers could decay or his reputation decline filled him with wrathful dismay. Caricature of himself, no matter how delicate or how comic, he could not endure. His personal peculiarities were to be held sacred, and no one must laugh at them; yet, unhappily, some of them were among the most laughable of comic attributes. Of self-poise, conscious rectitude, patience, and submission he did not possess a particle. Nor was his intellect broad enough to afford him consolation under the wounds that his vanity so often received. All his resource was to shut himself up in a kind of feudal retreat and grim seclusion, where he brooded upon himself as a great genius misunderstood, and upon the rest of the world as a sort of animated scum. That was an unlovely nature; but mingled in it were the comprehension and the incipient love of goodness, sweetness, beauty, and beneficent ideas. He vaguely knew what he had missed, whether of intellectual grandeur, moral excellence, or the happiness of the affections, and in the solitude of his spirit he brooded upon his misery. The sense of this commended him to sympathy when he was living and it should commend his memory to respect.

Both nature and fortune were kind to Edwin Forrest. He had a splendid physical constitution, rare qualities of tempera-

ment, and mental faculties of a more than
common worth. His lot was cast in a
country where it is possible for the poor to
rise. The hardships that befell him came
in youth, at a time of life when hardships
can best be borne, and when they are of
the most service; nor were they more
severe than such as have been met and
overcome by hundreds of other men, often
less fitted than he was to conquer them.
He had scarcely reached early manhood
before he attracted the admiring attention
of the public, in a pursuit which was congenial to him, and for which he was fitted;
and after that he speedily acquired both
fame and wealth. The honours that he
coveted were not withheld. Although there
were always persons who neither admired,
nor liked, nor praised him, yet no man in
America ever attracted larger crowds of
admirers, or elicited more copious and emphatic adulation. He was married to a
handsome and accomplished gentlewoman,
one who had mind and tact as well as manners and beauty. He possessed affectionate
and loyal friends — men such as William
Leggett and James Oakes — who stood by
him, with unshaken fondness and fidelity,
as long as they lived. He reached a pro-

fessional position where he could command
his own terms. He suffered from no lack
of organs of public opinion to celebrate,
expound, or defend him. There was no reason in the world, outside of himself, why
he should not have lived a triumphant and
happy life. Yet his existence was a tempest and his career a magnificent failure.

The wreck of Forrest's life was mainly
the result of Forrest's own character. Hard
and bitter circumstances once created of
course reacted upon him; but, in the main,
it was his character that first created them.
In youth he revolted against wholesome
discipline. In manhood he revolted against
culture, the restraints of good breeding
and social custom, the duty of consideration for other people, the supremacy of
spiritual law, and even those iron dictates
of destiny which, for each individual, flow
out of personality. He was constitutionally
a savage and always in rebellion. It has been
said of him that he was "born to rule and be
obeyed"—but no man can ever be fit to
rule others who cannot rule himself. Forrest
was always the slave of his ignorance, his
passion, and his prejudice, and was always
in a fume over his own limitations. He had
just knowledge enough to know that there

is such a thing as learning, and he resented, with fierce aversion, the nevertheless irrefutable fact that this was possessed by others that was not possessed by him. He believed himself to be a man of genius, but to his mind this meant that he was unlike other men, and superior to them, and therefore ordained and privileged to dominate everything. The actor temperament, in the nature of things often selfish, was in him selfishness incarnate. He recognised neither fault in his character nor error in his conduct. He either could not or would not subject himself to restraint. In adversity he was not humble; in prosperity he was not modest. Towards his professional associates, unless he liked them or unless he was met with unabashed spirit, his demeanour was often arrogant, tyrannical, and offensive. He liked to feel his royal authority and to make the weak tremble. He could, indeed, be magnanimous, loving, and kind — for he was human and had warmth as well of the affections as of the passions; and it is known that he did gentle and charitable acts. But nothing like self-government, nothing like philosophic or dutiful submission, nothing like humble acceptance of the chastening lessons of experience, appeared in any important moment of his life. His first thought at such times was of his own vast and overwhelming self. He was proud, self-assertive, and perfectly ravenous of praise, power, and money. Love for the dramatic art, at first an instinct, soon became in him a vain appetite; he loved it because it was a means of personal glorification. When he went abroad to act — a young man of only thirty — he was "the celebrated Mr. Forrest, the eminent American tragedian." Bounce and bluster. When he found his acting of Spartacus liked, he at once assumed national proportions, crystallising the United States into himself, and publicly approving of the English people for their tribute to the American Republic. He insulted Macready, in the manner of a rowdy, and without the slightest reason or justification. Somebody had disparaged his acting, when in London; that somebody must have been hired by Macready to do it; Macready was therefore a scoundrel; the aristocracy of Great Britain and the literary prigs in general had conspired to offend the pet of the prairie; and it was necessary to have a row. From no motive better than the spiteful resentment of wounded vanity did Forrest foment the evil passions which at last broke forth in the sanguinary riot in Astor Place. When his domestic trouble came the same boisterous animal fury flamed out with renewed violence. He was neither reticent nor decent. The idea of privately bearing his private burdens seems never to have occurred to him. Another ache had arrived to the great Forrest, and another row must give it an adequate celebration. He brought against his wife the vilest of charges in the foulest of words. He threw to the winds all discretion and sense. He kept up for years a theatrical scandal which was a public nuisance and a crying shame. His behaviour all through that self-inflicted ordeal was that of an unreasoning beast. He personally villified and vituperated Charles O'Conor. He thrashed N. P. Willis. He professionally ostracised and ruined George Jamieson. He tried to do the same thing with John Gilbert. Not an actor who did not espouse his cause could come into the same theatre with him. He threw off his best and most powerful friends. Once aroused, there was no end to his suspicion and no limit to his violent cruelty. Those are facts of common knowledge. No man can be deemed a great character whose dominant idea in life is the announcement, aggrandisement, and celebration of himself, or who, in the patient, thorough, far-seeing pursuit of duty, is incapable of foregoing, easily and cheerfully, the praise of other men. Had mankind been made up of melodious flunkeys, with their trumpets well polished and in a state of everlasting toot, Forrest would probably have been content. As it was, he continued, to the last, growling over the idea that something had been withheld from him that the world ought to have given. He was a great man, and somebody had said that he was not. He was the greatest actor that ever lived, and some scurrilous newspaper in Podunk had denied it. He was Timon scowling along Broadway; he was Lear parading in Chestnut street; and the miserable human race would not be awed by the spectacle. There was always a fly in his ointment, a Mordecai at his gate, sullen resentment in his heart, and scorn on his lips. Such a man is picturesque as a ruin and becomes a study for the curious, but he is far from being either noble or salutary. Such a character, perhaps, is more to be pitied than blamed; but such is not the kind of character for which the reverence of the world can successfully be invoked. When a man poses as a genius and a martyr, and invites the admiration and sympathy of the world, the world is apt to inquire what he has done and what ails him. Byron, gloomily sequestered in his Venetian palace and consumed at heart with the strife between his inherent goodness and his inherent evil, had at least written *Childe Harold* and *Manfred*. Those were immortal productions, destined to charm and elevate the human mind as long as time shall endure. Forrest added no such treasure to the store of human benefits, even in his pursuit of the stage. He was a successful actor, in a certain school ; but his school was not the highest and he was not its best representative. He came out in 1826. He had seen Cooper and he was presently associated with Edmund Kean ; and on those two actors his style was modelled — with a stronger inclination toward the former than the latter. His physical attributes determined his course. He inherited the traditions of Cooke and Cooper. He was never — if the conclusions of reading can be trusted — the equal of either of them ; he, certainly, never carried the art of acting to a higher pitch of excellence than it had reached when they left it. The thing wherein he was peculiar, the distinguishing excellence that gave him his victory and made him memorable, was a puissant animal splendour and ground-swell of emotion. He was tremendously real. He could be seen and heard and understood. He had a grand body and a glorious voice, and in moments of simple passion he affected the senses like the blare of trumpets and clash of cymbals, or like the ponderous, slow-moving, crashing, and thundering surges of the sea. In that quality he stood alone. In all others he has been surpassed. That was his charm, and through that he was enabled to render whatever service he did render to the cause of the drama.

That service consisted in a widespread, delightful, and improving interpretation of the art of acting to the lower order of public intelligence. To the higher order of mind Forrest was superfluous; and of this fact he seemed, in a certain blind way, to be aware —although neither he nor any one of his adherents could understand and believe that it was possible for any person, honestly and without hostility or prejudice, to dis-

like the snorts and grunts, the brays and
belches, the gaspings and gurglings, the
protracted pauses, the lolling tongue and
the stentorian roar, with all of which orna-
ments it pleased him to overlay his acting
— often remarkably fine and sometimes
great. In acting, as in poetry, there are,
popularly, two schools. One is the Rossetti ; the other is the Walt Whitman. The
one is all for spirit ; the other is all for body.
The Rossetti would be a disembodied soul,
floating in through the keyhole and hovering
over a Dresden teacup. The Whitman ex-
ults in flesh. The eclectic school, which is the
right school, — in acting and in every other
art, — stands between those extremes and
simply asks the harmonious and symmetrical blending of the spiritual and physical.
Our ancestors had that, in Garrick and
Kemble ; we have it in Edwin Booth and
Henry Irving. Neither of these latter actors
is equal with Forrest in his distinctive element ; but each has excelled him in fine
mentality, in spirituality, and in poetry.

VI.

LIFE AND CHARACTER OF GILBERT.

1810 — 1889.

THE death of John Gilbert [June 17, 1889, at Boston], although an event rationally to be expected — for he was close on eighty years of age — came upon the community with a peculiar sense of grief. The actor, the gentleman, the friend had lived with us a long time and had become entwined with precious memories and associations. The grand figures with which we have been familiar are vanishing, one by one. The institutions and the ways of our personal world are breaking up around us. New men and new ideas and interests are thrusting aside the broken fragments of our past. The shadows darken around us. A little later we shall be shadows ourselves. The death of John Gilbert marked an epoch in the experience of the generation that is passing away — solemnly warning it of its own decline. It marked also an

epoch in the history of the American stage;
for John Gilbert had been an actor for close
on sixty-one years, and within his time the
art of acting [exemplifying its customary
periodicity of flow and ebb] had risen to a
climax, and had begun to wane.

John Gibbs Gilbert was a native of Boston, born February 27, 1810. His birth
occurred in a house in Richmond street,
next to that in which Charlotte Cushman
was born, and those two — afterward so
famous actors — were playmates in child-
hood. Gilbert went on the stage in his
nineteenth year, making his first appearance
November 28, 1828, at the Tremont theatre,
in Boston. The play was Otway's tragedy
of *Venice Preserved,* and Gilbert acted
Jaffier. The Belvidera was Mary Duff —
one of the best actresses that ever adorned
the stage — a woman as eminent in her day
as Cushman and Ristori have been in our
time, and worthy to be remembered with
the most illustrious of dramatic artists.
His next characters were Sir Edward Mortimer, in *The Iron Chest*, and Shakespeare's
Shylock. He continued for the rest of the
season of 1828 to act at the Tremont theatre,
taking all parts that were cast to him; but
in the fall of that year he joined the com-

pany at the Camp-street theatre, New
Orleans, under Caldwell's management, and
during the ensuing five years he acted with
that troop, sometimes in New Orleans,
sometimes in towns on the Mississippi
river — playing all sorts of parts, but
gradually drifting into the line of old men.
On his return to Boston, in 1834, he again
came forward at the Tremont theatre, acting Mr. Dornton, in *The Road to Ruin*.
The occasion was that of a benefit to George
Barrett — a favorite comedian of that
epoch. The Tremont was then managed
by Thomas Barry — [who died on February 11, 1876, full of years and honours].
Gilbert was at once engaged there, and
there he remained for the next five years.
His line of parts at that time comprised
tragedy as well as comedy, but his tendency was toward the specialty of first
old men — in which for many years he
had no equal and scarcely a rival. Blake
was the only actor of his time who ever
surpassed him in that line, and Blake could
excel him only in certain unctuous parts or
in parts of great tenderness. The versatility of his talents and the variety of his
efforts at that time are denoted by the list
of parts which he acted during the first

season with Barry. This includes Master Walter, Isaac of York, Sir Peter Teazle, Pizarro, Iago, Sir Edward Mortimer, Admiral Kingston, Lieutenant Worthington, Sir Robert Bramble, Polonius, Uncle John, Tom Noddy, Macduff, Mr. Dornton, Squeers, Henry the Sixth, Adam, Malec, Kent, and Rolanio. Barry relinquished the Tremont theatre after two seasons, and Dr. Jones, author of *Solon Shingle* and many other pieces, and long well known and popular in Boston, became its lessee. Gilbert was engaged as stage-manager and to act the same round of parts. Two seasons later the theatre passed into the hands of George H. Andrews, the comedian, for one year; but Dr. Jones resumed its management in the next year and wound up its affairs. Gilbert remained in it, and on its final night as a theatre he acted Sir Robert Bramble and pronounced a farewell address; so that he was the last actor who spoke upon the stage of the old Tremont. The building was purchased by a church society, and being rented for lectures, with theatrical scenery, it was reopened with a hymn, beginning "Lord, let these ransomed walls rejoice!"

A little while previous to the disruption of the Tremont Gilbert acted at the Bow-

ery theatre, New York — under Hamblin's
management — having been engaged to
personate the sexton, Peter Bradley, in
Rookwood. He made his first appearance
there, however, as Sir Edward Mortimer.
His next engagement after the Tremont
closed was at Pelby's National, in Boston — the only theatre then open in that
city. From there he went to the Federal-
street theatre, when that once-famous
house — long since swept away — was reopened by Oliver C. Wyman, and on that
occasion he spoke the opening address,
written by Frances Sargent Osgood. The
season was disastrous and it closed in March
1846. In April, that year, Gilbert went to
London for a little rest ; but, being asked to
act, he appeared at the Princess's theatre as
Sir Robert Bramble, and he was cordially
received by the public and the press ; whereupon he accepted an engagement at the
Princess's theatre for the next season. The
interim he passed in Paris, where he saw
and studied the artists of the Théâtre Fran-
çais — Rachel, Rose Chéri, Lafont, Frederick Lemaître, Bocage, Fechter, and others.
Then he acted for one season at the Princess's in London, and then returned home.
He is next found at the Park theatre, in

New York, where he came forward as Sir
Anthony Absolute, and where he remained
till the destruction of that house by fire —
December 16, 1848. He spoke the last words
that were ever uttered on that stage, acting
Admiral Kingston in *Naval Engagements*.
Hamblin then engaged him at the Bowery,
which in those days was a theatre of the
best class and possessed a capital dramatic
company, including Mr. and Mrs. James
W. Wallack, Jr., Lester Wallack, Miss
Wemyss, Mary Taylor, and others of local
renown. There he remained some time;
but he is presently found at the Howard
Athenæum, Boston, and later at the Chest-
nut-street theatre, Philadelphia. At the
latter he remained till the opening of the
Boston theatre, in 1854, when he was again
engaged by Barry. On the opening night
of that theatre he spoke the address written
by that rare poet T. W. Parsons, and acted
Sir Anthony Absolute. Four consecutive
seasons found him constant in his duties at
that theatre and growing more and more in
the affectionate respect of the Boston public.
He played the old men almost exclusively;
yet he was now seen in two of the most widely contrasted and difficult characters in the
range of the drama — Bottom and Caliban.

"The humour of Gilbert's performance of Bottom," said a critical authority of the time, "was exquisite. The egregious vanity in the casting of the play — the bottomless vanity and Bottomish ignorance — were never more faithfully denoted. It had the true Shakespearean flavour." Another critical writer said : "Gilbert's Caliban is a great personation. Of itself and by itself it is just as good in its way as anything Forrest or Brooke or Wallack can accomplish. It is a finished and elaborate yet very vigorous exhibition of dramatic ability ; and those who have not seen it are not aware of what John Gilbert is capable, although they may be thoroughly conversant with his Philip Sabois, Rolanio, Sir Peter Teazle, Sir Anthony Absolute, and half a hundred other parts that he gives so delicately and so naturally." At one of his benefits in Boston, during that fertile and brilliant period of his professional life, Gilbert received a public gift of a costly service of silver plate. It was during his stay at the Boston theatre that Edwin Forrest, who was his enemy, paid him the compliment of invariably stipulating, in the written contracts under which the tragedian came there to play star engagements, that John Gilbert should not appear in any performance given by him. This was because Gilbert had approved of the cause of Mrs. Forrest, in the once notorious divorce suit.

From the Boston theatre, in 1858, the comedian went to the Arch in Philadelphia, and there he remained till engaged by the elder Wallack, for the house opened by him in Broadway, at the corner of Thirteenth street, in 1861. Gilbert came forward as Sir Peter Teazle, and at once established himself in the admiration of the New-York public. He remained attached to Wallack's theatre until it ceased to exist — in 1888. From him chiefly the passing generation of playgoers received its knowledge of the best traditions of the stage, as associated with the old men of the old comedies ; and their recollections of those subjects are intertwined with his honoured name.

Gilbert was twice married, but he left no children. His first wife was Miss Campbell, a native of Philadelphia, born in 1806. With her he wedded in 1836. That lady became an actress, appearing at the Tremont theatre, Boston, as Sophie, in *Of Age Tomorrow*, and on March 15, 1842, at the Bowery theatre, New York, as Old Lady Lambert, in *The Hypocrite*. She visited

England with her husband in 1846, and was
seen at the Princess's theatre, as Mrs. Lily-
white in *Forty or Fifty*. Her death occurred
on April 27, 1866, in New York, and she
was buried near Boston. Gilbert subsequently espoused Sarah H. Gavett, of Boston, who survived him. In his married life,
as in all other ways, he was fortunate and
happy. I have been with him in his home,
at Manchester-by-the-Sea, and I remember
it as the favoured abode of affection and
peace.

The long annals of the British stage are
opened the moment you begin to review
Gilbert's achievements, to analyse his art,
and to consider his professional rank.
Quin, Dowton, Munden, Liston, Reeves,
Farren, Burton, Blake, Hackett, Burke,
and Bass are some of the renowned names
which start up in imagination or remembrance, as the ancestry or brotherhood of
that remarkable man. How full John Gilbert's professional life was of endeavour,
how high in quality, and therefore how re-
fining and elevating in influence, equally
upon his own character and upon the public mind, may be gathered from a glance
at some of the parts he played. The list
includes King John, Hubert, King Philip,

Cardinal Pandulph, Sir Peter Teazle, Sir
Oliver Surface, Crabtree, Rowley, Sir An-
thony Absolute, Kit Cosey, Sir William
Dorrilon, Lord Pleony, Sir William Fond-
love, Sir John Falstaff, Justice Woodcock,
Malvolio, Polonius, The Ghost of King
Hamlet, Dogberry, Adam, Leontes, Anti-
gonus, Autolycus, Mr. Simpson, Lord Du-
berley, Tom Noddy, Captain Copp, Colonel
Hardy, Governor Heartall, Sir Bashful Con-
stant, Lord Ogleby, Dr. Cantwell, Sir
Robert Bramble, Sir Francis Gripe, Squeers,
Mr. Dombey, Justice Greedy, Colonel
Damas, Admiral Kingston, Don Manuel,
Mr. Hardcastle, Shylock, Sir Edward Mor-
timer, Dr. Dilworth, Sir Paul Pagoda, Sir
Paladin Scruple, Sir Hartcourt Courtley,
Sarcasm, Dominie Sampson, Baillie Nicol
Jarvie, Sir Alexander Shendryn, Penrud-
dock, Adrastus, Iago, Master Walter,
Matthew Elmore, Henry VIII., Cardinal
Wolsey, Jacques, Adam Brock, Old Norval,
Job Thornberry, Jesse Rural, Menenius,
Adam Winterton, Mr. Dowton, Old Rapid,
Mr. Aspen, Mr. Coddle, Macbeth, all the
parts in the tragedy of *Macbeth*, except
Lady Macbeth and the waiting gentle-
woman, and all the parts in *Julius Cæsar*,
except the boy Lucius. That is but a tithe

of the veteran's achievement; yet it lays bare the springs of that renown which was the pride of John Gilbert's contemporaries and friends, and which will adorn and illumine the annals of dramatic history.

Formal but not severe, stately without pomp, dignified without severity, formidable in its self-reliance and reticence, individual, positive, scrupulous and exact, but neither aggressive nor caustic, the personality of John Gilbert, although it impressed many of his acquaintances as exclusive and cold, was sincere, manly, gentle, and even tender. He had strong convictions. He was uncompromising. He never flattered anybody, and he never assumed a cordiality that he did not feel. His manner was usually urbane, but his temper was impetuous, and when offended by frivolity, professional incompetence, or sychophantic fawning, — three things which especially he detested, — he could express contempt and scorn with energetic indignation and righteous vehemence. The profession of the actor was, in his esteem, sacred. He allowed no levity on that subject, and his anger was quickly aroused by any trifling with the dramatic art. "Acting, sir," he said to me, on one occasion, — and he wrote

the same thought on another, — "is often
called a matter of opinion or of taste ; it is
nothing of the kind — it is a matter of fact."
His meaning was that a competent actor
gives a performance that is correct and
right, and that its merit is independent of
preference or caprice. He knew his art
thoroughly, in every department of it and
in every particular, and no one could teach
him anything about it, — willing though
he was to learn, and always deferential to
the authority of true intellect and honest
thought. He perfectly understood, furthermore, the scope and the nature of his own
abilities ; so that, in his riper years, he
never willingly undertook what he was
unfitted to achieve, and he never failed to
do well whatever he undertook to do at all.
The traditions of the stage were known to
him and he respected them — maintaining
that they are the fruits of experience, and
are rational and wise. Innovations were
obnoxious to his judgment. The modern
juvenile actor who plies the conspicuous
wrist-band, poses on the hearth-rug, and
continually toys with the incombustible
cigar, impressed him as a vacuous impertinence. He required strong and distinct
character, a definite ideal clearly expressed ;

fidelity to the text; accuracy in apparel; absolute concurrence with the manners of the time and of the society to be depicted; imagination and sensibility in treatment; harmonious concentration of all the parts and elements in a performance; and pure and perfect use of the language. Those things he invariably gave when he acted; and even toward the last, when his faculties had begun to fail, he seldom strayed from that absolute precision which for fifty years had been the conspicuous excellence of his art. The actor whom he most admired was Macready — a man of exalted genius, who preferred to pursue a severely accurate method rather than to depend upon the capricious gusts of inspiration. Macready in Richelieu, William Tell, Werner, Virginius, and Macbeth he declared to be perfection — never within his knowledge surpassed or even rivalled. What he thus admired it was natural that he should emulate. He was sometimes a great actor; he was always a correct one. In such characters as Sir Sampson Legend and Sir Anthony Absolute no man of his time approached him, and it is doubtful whether, in that line of individuality, he was ever equalled. Those are unlovely characters, tyrannical

and choleric, and they evoked only a part
of the constituents of his ample and comprehensive nature. He acted them with
ease and he was perfect in them, but for
the fuller expression of his nature you had
to see him as Sir Peter Teazle, Sir Robert
Bramble, Jesse Rural, and above all as Mr.
Dornton. The personations that he gave
of those parts revealed the tenderness of
his heart and the lovely refinement of his
mind, commingled with a strain of humour
which was now jocular, now whimsical,
and at all times — certainly within the last
fifteen or twenty years of his professional
life — spontaneous, genial, and fluent. He
had been a hard actor. He gave, for example, the best performance of Caliban
that ever was seen in America — and there
was in his method all that this fact denotes.
But that quality of hardness gradually wore
away, and in the latter part of his career
he was never so fine as in characters of a
venerable aspect, a gentle temperament,
and a soft, benign, and winning manner.
One of the best of his achievements was the
embodiment of the Abbé Constantin, which
he gave when his days were nearly ended.
In the garden of his heart the last flowers
that bloomed were still the sweetest, because
they were the flowers of charity and love.

VII.

SKETCH OF JOHN BROUGHAM.

1810 — 1880.

THE life of John Brougham (who died, June 7, 1880, at No. 60 East Ninth street, New York), notable for many things, was especially remarkable for two qualities — its brilliancy and its goodness. Fifty years of it he passed upon the stage ; and, both as actor and author, his influence always tended to gladden and sweeten the human experience of which he was a part. The reason of this was that within the actor and author there was a true man. His heart was large, warm, and charitable ; his mind was eager, hopeful, cheerful, and actively creative ; his instincts were virtuous and kindly ; his temperament was gentle ; and his consideration for others — which extended to the humblest of living creatures, was thoughtful of the most minute point of delicacy, found excuse for every fault, and gave forgiveness for almost every wrong —

sprang from the spontaneous desire that
everybody should be happy. His thoughts,
and often his talk, dwelt upon the great
disparity of conditions in society, the struggles and sufferings of the poor, and the
relation of evil to the infirmities of human
nature. He did not live for himself alone,
but he was profoundly and practically interested in others; and that feeling, as
potent as it was genuine, animated all his
life, coloured all his work, and so commended him to the responsive sympathy
and good-will of his generation that his
name, on every lip, was the name of a
friend.

In his writings as in his acting the characteristic quality was a sort of off-hand
dash and glittering merriment, a commingling of bluff, breezy humour with
winning manliness. The atmosphere of
his art was always that of sincerity, but
it never had the insipidity of strenuous
goodness. He was intellectual, and at
times poetic and romantic; but he was
human and he was gay, and he loved to
adorn life with the Celtic sparkle. His
rich, rolling voice, with a touch of the
brogue in it, sounds in all he wrote, and
his happy, infectious laughter, for all who

recall his acting, will echo in memory as long as they live. The scope and variety of his labours were great. He threw himself with the keenest zest into the passing moment; he dreaded no task; he shunned no emergency; he attempted all sorts of composition, to which either his agile fancy impelled him, or which the need of the hour exacted; and, while he was not equally successful in every line of literature, or every walk of the stage, he produced a surprising number of effective dramas, and he acted many and diversified parts in an admirable manner. During the first twenty years of his life — which were passed in and around the city of Dublin, where he was born May 9, 1810 — he was provided with opportunities of liberal education; and those he improved, acquiring knowledge, however, as he has said of himself, rather by absorption than application; and all his life he was a reader and a student; so that his labours were based on a solid foundation of good mental discipline. In other words, he was a scholar; and the operations of his mind, however impulsive and erratic they sometimes may have been, were usually guided and restrained by that knowledge of the intellectual field, and that

sense of proportion and harmony, of fitness
and of taste, which only scholarship can
give.

He began life as a student of surgery, and
for several months walked the Peter-street
hospital, Dublin; but a sudden stroke of
adversity deprived him of the prospect of
fortune, and threw him upon his own resources, and he thereupon went up to London, and by chance became an actor. This
was an accident; for, when destitute of
money, he had offered himself as a cadet in
the East India Company's service, and had
only been restrained from enlisting by the
recruiting officer, — a stranger, but a kind
old man, — who gave him a guinea and
urged him to seek some other and fitter
employment. A chance encounter with an
old acquaintance, within an hour or two
after that incident occurred, led to his
engagement at what was then the Totten-
ham-street theatre, afterward the Prince of
Wales; and there, in July 1830 acting six
characters in the rough play of *Tom and
Jerry*, he began that sparkling professional
career which now is only a memory. In
1831 he was a member of the company
organised by Madame Vestris for the London Olympic, and his name appears in

the cast of *Olympic Revels* [Mars, Mr. Brougham] in the first full bill issued by that once famous manager. From the Olympic he made professional trips into the provinces, and played all sorts of parts. His first play was written at that time, and was a burlesque, prepared for William E. Burton, who then was acting in London, at the Pavilion theatre. When Vestris removed from the Olympic to Covent Garden, Brougham followed her thither, and there he remained as long as Vestris and Charles Mathews were at the head of the theatre; and it was while there that [as he always claimed] he co-operated with Dion Boucicault in writing the comedy of *London Assurance.*

In 1840 he became manager of the London Lyceum, which he conducted during summer seasons, and he wrote for production at that home *Life in the Clouds, Love's Livery, Enthusiasm, Tom Thumb the Second,* and, in conjunction with Mark Lemon, *The Demon Gift.*

His American career began in 1842, when, as O'Callaghan, in *His Last Legs,* he came forward at the old Park theatre, in New York. Those days, he said, were "the palmy days of light houses and heavy gas-bills." A starring tour of the country followed, and, incidentally, the comedian lost all his earnings, while endeavouring, aboard a Mississippi river steamboat, to learn the national game of "draw poker." A little later he was employed in Burton's company, in New York, and for Burton he wrote *Bunsby's Wedding*, *The Confidence Man*, *Don Cæsar de Bassoon*, *Vanity Fair*, *The Irish Yankee*, *Benjamin Franklin*, *All's Fair in Love*, *The Irish Emigrant*, and a play on *Dombey and Son*. Still later he managed Niblo's Garden, producing there his fairy tale called *Home*, and the play of *Ambrose Germain*, written for Mlle. Blangy. On December 23, 1850, he opened Brougham's Lyceum, in Broadway, near the south-west corner of Broome street; and while there he wrote *The World's Fair*, *Faustus*, *The Spirit of Air*, *Row at the Lyceum*, a dramatisation of *David Copperfield*, and a new version of *The Actress of Padua*, — the latter for Charlotte Cushman. The demolition of the building next to his theatre, however, made it appear to be unsafe, and so his business which had begun well, was seriously injured; and he always said that the misdealing of a false friend took that property out of his hands

and left him burdened with debt — all of
which, however, he subsequently paid.   In
theatrical management he was always unfortunate — partly because he always acted
from principle and never from expediency,
partly because he would not consider the
caprices of public taste, and partly because
he was gentle and yielding in nature.

From the Lyceum — which afterwards
became Wallack's theatre, and so remained
till 1860 — he went to the Bowery (July 7,
1856), where he revived *King John*, with
superb scenery by Hilliard, and with a cast
that included Edwin L. Davenport, Mrs.
Davenport, William Wheatley, J. B. Howe,
and Kate Reignolds ; but that did not succeed, and he then wrote and produced a
large number of Bowery dramas, among
which were *The Pirates of the Mississippi*,
The Red Mask, — based on a current tale
called *The Gun-Maker of Moscow*, — *Orion,
the Gold Beater*, *Tom and Jerry in America*,
and *The Miller of New Jersey*.   He then
accepted employment in Wallack's company, and, for "the veteran's" theatre,
wrote *The Game of Love*, a version of
Bleak House, *My Cousin German*, *A Decided Case*, *The Game of Life*, the famous
burlesque of *Pocahontas*, *Neptune's Defeat*,

*Love and Murder, Romance and Reality,
The Ruling Passion,* and *Playing With
Fire*. After several seasons at Wallack's
he rejoined Burton — then at the Metropoli-
tan theatre, formerly Tripler hall, and
finally the Winter Garden, in Broadway,
nearly opposite to Bond street, — and there
he produced his burlesque of *Columbus,
This House to Be Sold,* and several other
plays. In September 1860 he went to
England, where he remained five years.
While there he adapted from the French,
for Fechter, *The Duke's Motto,* and *Bel
Demonio,* and wrote, for Miss Herbert,
dramatic versions of *Lady Audley's Secret*
and *Only a Clod*. He also wrote *While
There's Life There's Hope,* acted at the
Strand; *The Might of Right,* acted at
Astley's; *The Golden Dream,* produced at
Manchester; the words of three operas:
Blanche de Nevers, The Demon Lovers, and
The Bride of Venice; several songs and
poems, and several pieces of music, one of
which, *The Bob-o-Link Polka,* subsequently
became popular. His comedy of *Playing
With Fire* was produced at the Princess's
theatre, and he himself acted there, and
also at the Lyceum. His reappearance in
America was effected on October 30, 1865,

at the Winter Garden theatre, and he never afterwards went abroad. He acted in a round of parts at that time, beginning with Dr. Savage, and continuing with Foxglove, in his own *Flies in the Web*, Powhatan, Columbus, and McShane, in *The Nervous Man and the Man of Nerve*, and he wound up the engagement, which lasted three months, with his drama of *O'Donnell's Mission*, in which he acted Roderick O'Donnell.

In February 1867 a new piece by Brougham, entitled *The Christian Martyrs*, was produced at Barnum's Museum, and in May of the same year he filled a brief engagement at the Olympic, appearing as O'Donnell, Captain Cuttle, Micawber, and Powhatan. In the following August he again played there, and at the same time his drama of *Little Nell and the Marchioness*, written for Lotta [Miss Charlotte Crabtree], was brought out at Wallack's theatre (August 14, 1867). In the summer of 1868 he produced, at the Walnut in Philadelphia, *Hearts; or, The Serpents of Society*, and on June 8, in that year, he brought forward, at Wallack's theatre, his melodrama of *The Lottery of Life*, and himself acted the chief part. This had a run of nine weeks.

In December, that year, his play of *The Emerald Ring*, written for Barney Williams, was produced at the Broadway theatre —Wallack's old house — which Williams then managed. On January 25, 1869, he opened Brougham's theatre, on the site of what is now the Madison-square theatre, with a comedy by himself, called *Better Late Than Never*, — in which he acted Major Fergus O'Shaughnessy, — and *The Dramatic Review for 1868*. He subsequently produced an adaptation called *Irish Stew*, and his capital burlesque, in which he used to act Shylock, entitled *Much Ado About a Merchant of Venice*. That theatre was taken out of his hands by its unscrupulous owner, and on April 3 Brougham closed his season with a performance of *His Last Legs*. On April 4 a banquet in his honour was given at the Astor House, and on May 18 he received a farewell benefit — performances being given at the theatre which is now called the Fourteenth street, and at Niblo's theatre. The attempt to establish Brougham's theatre was his final effort in management. After that time he was connected with various stock companies, but chiefly with Daly's theatre and with Wallack's. Among his later works may be

mentioned *The Red Light*, in which he
acted at Wallack's theatre, June 6, 1870,
Minnie's Luck, produced at the same house,
John Garth, given at Wallack's, December
12, 1871; *The Lily of France*, brought out
December 16, 1872, at Booth's theatre, by
Miss Helen Temple, who enacted Joan of
Arc, and *Slander*, and *Good-Bye*, in which
he made his last professional tour of the
country, in the fall of 1877. In 1852
Brougham edited a bright, comic paper in
New York, called *The Lantern*, and he
published two collections of his miscella-
neous writings, entitled *A Basket of Chips*,
and *The Bunsby Papers*. On January 17,
1878, he received a testimonial benefit at
the Academy of Music, at which the sum
of $10,278.56 was received; and that fund,
after payment of the incidental expenses,
was settled on him, in an annuity, — which
expired at his death. It was thought that
he would live for many years, and the
desire and design of his friends, in the
arrangement then made, was to insure his
protection from want, in his old age. He
began, years ago, the composition of an
Autobiography, at the earnest solicitation
of a friend [the present writer], but this
remains unfinished. His last work was a

drama entitled *Home Rule*, in which he treated political and social affairs in Ireland. His last appearance on the stage was made as Felix O'Reilly, a detective, in Dion Boucicault's play of *Rescued*, at Booth's theatre, New York, October 25, 1879.

The recital of these facts is indicative of the current of his career, the great vitality and industry by which it was marked, and the variable success with which it was crowned. Actors, more than most of the persons who live by their efforts in the realm of art, are necessarily affected by the immediate influences of their time. Their characters, in other words, are, to a considerable extent, bent and molded by public opinion and caprice. They feel the necessity of the instant response; and, accordingly, they are not slow to make that direct appeal in which very often there is more of impulse than of judgment, the tinsel of artifice rather than the pure gold of art. Brougham, like many of his contemporaries, recognised this necessity; but his sincerity of feeling, his sturdiness of character, his scholar-like taste, and his intense loyalty to the higher principles and best ideals of art were all combined in antagonism to worldly prudence and expediency; and, all through the story of his life, it is easy to trace, not merely a roving, drifting, careless disposition, — the light-hearted heedlessness and yielding amiability of Goldsmith, whom, in some ways he resembled, — but the resolute bent of a mind that spontaneously insisted on going its own way and fulfilling its own laws. There was, indeed, in his intellectual endeavour, no continuity of movement towards a definite goal, clearly seen afar off. But he was born to be a man of letters, a poetic artist, and a wit, and he could not, except in a fitful manner, take his cue from his circumstances. His experience, therefore, was often that of conflict with prevailing fashions, and, towards the last, of considerable spiritual discontent.

The fact that fortune always, sooner or later, slipped through his fingers was, doubtless, chiefly ascribable to his buoyant Hibernian recklessness of the ordinary precautions of prudence, and to his heedless trust in everybody. He adapted *The Duke's Motto* for Fechter, for instance, and it had a prosperous career in London ; but all that he ever received for his work upon it was a box of cigars ; and with transactions of that kind his whole business career was spangled. But, even with a harder temperament, he

would still have been at odds with the practical spirit of his time. He had originality
as a man, even more than as a writer, and
he was often a dreamer in the midst of the
battle. Those of his dramatic works in
which he himself took the most pleasure,
and in which the student will hereafter discern the most of the man, are the burlesque
of *Columbus*, the blank-verse drama of *The
Lily of France*, and the comedy of *Playing
With Fire*. They contain delicate thought,
poetic suggestion, sweet-tempered satire,
contemplative philosophy, and pathos. He
often chose to appear to be, in a mild and
elegant way, "the rantin' roarin' Irish-
man"; he was, in fact, nothing of the kind,
but a pensive moralist, a poetic dreamer, a
delicate, sensitive gentleman, as frank and
honest as a child, and as gentle as a woman.

His rank among actors it is difficult to
assign. He excelled in humour rather than
in pathos or sentiment, and was at his best
in the expression of comically eccentric
character. Among the parts that will live
in memory, as associated with his name,
are Stout in *Money*, Dennis Brulgruddery
in *John Bull*, Sir Lucius O'Trigger in
The Rivals, Cuttle, Micawber, Bagstock,
O'Grady in *Arrah-Na-Pogue*, Dazzle in

London Assurance, Captain Murphy Maguire in *The Serious Family*, and O'Callaghan in *His Last Legs.* His animal spirits, dash, vigour, and brilliancy in those parts were great ; he entered deeply into their spirit ; he could be consciously joyous or unconsciously droll ; he was not for an instant out of the stage picture ; and he spoke the language with delicious purity. He gave an immense amount of pleasure ; he did no harm ; he went to his grave in the fulness of years and honours ; his best works live after him, in the usage of the stage and the admiration of the public ; he was deeply mourned ; and it will be a long time before any one who ever knew him can speak, without a sigh, the name of John Brougham.

His talk of old times was deeply interesting, full of anecdote, and various with sketches of character, witty comment, and professional learning. He had seen Munden and Liston and many another worthy of the old school. He knew Charles Mathews in his youth, and could have traced the whole growth of that sparkling mind and vigorous career which finally became so famous. He saw the incidents which attended Sir Walter Scott's last sojourn in

London, when that intellectual giant was forced to pause there, as he was going home to die. He was familiar with the last days of Campbell and Rogers, and contemporary with the opening careers of both Dickens and Thackeray. He was the comrade of Dion Boucicault when that author was little more than a boy. His memories of the Kembles and the Keans were perfectly distinct, and his descriptions of Macready and of Charles Kean in particular — with both of whom he had acted, and for both of whom he had managed the stage — were remarkably humorous and not a little pungent with drollery. To hear his account of a performance by Charles Kean, with all the people about the stage shod in list slippers, was to realise a truthful and instructive picture and to enjoy a complete exhilaration. He possessed an unerring faculty of mimicry; and, as he said, "you take my life when you do take the *beans* whereby I live," the listener heard again the living voice of Charles Kean. In felicity of theatrical anecdote there has been no one like him since George Jamieson and John Sefton, and in the simulation of unconsciously comic attributes he did not leave an equal among actors, aside from Chanfrau and Jefferson.

He touched many styles, but, as Johnson said of Goldsmith, he touched nothing that he did not adorn. Although he lived in the library and maintained and cherished a high ideal of what the literary artist should strive to accomplish, he had neither the erudite prosiness nor the exclusive isolation of the abstract scholar : he lived also in the world and with the life of his time. He clasped the hands of men and women ; he spoke to their hearts ; he was interested in their fortunes ; "their welfare pleased him and their cares distrest" ; and wherever he went he carried the benediction of good deeds and left the sunshine of love and laughter. Those persons who heard his off-hand speeches before the curtain will often call to mind what a ring of genuine kindness there was in his voice, what a light of geniality there was in his face, what a glow of animal spirits he diffused around him, what a winning ideal of manliness he suggested, — with his native elegance of bearing and the breezy heartiness and joyous dash of his manners. Those who were brought near to him in the business of life will not forget his thoughtful consideration, his delicate courtesy, his simple goodness. The poor had cause to bless him, though himself was poor. As he lay in his coffin, his noble face, grand in the awful serenity of death, was like the face of Shakespeare. The light, the merriment, the trouble, the pain, were all gone, and nothing but the majesty remained ; and looking on him there I thought of Shakespeare's words :

> "Our cause of sorrow
> Must not be measured by his worth, for then
> It hath no end."

VIII.

GEORGE W. JAMIESON.

1810 — 1868.

ON Tuesday afternoon, October 6, 1868, in the village of Yonkers, a few actors and other friends of George W. Jamieson assembled in the church of St. John to perform funeral rites over his remains and to lay them in the grave. The day was uncommonly sweet and beautiful — a peaceful autumn day, a day for sad thought and sadder parting. The mourners around the coffin of George Jamieson were not numerous, but they were sincere ; and his poor, bruised body was tenderly laid at rest by hands that in life he loved to grasp. He could not have wished a different funeral. His attachments, while living, were few, and no man could entertain a stronger aversion than was felt by him for the pretence of friendship or the vanity of ostentation. Suddenly and terribly his life came to an end. Sadly and simply his remains were borne to their place of final repose. His grave is in a little cemetery back of Yonkers. There he rests, after years of toil and of weary waiting, embittered by disappointment, sorrow, poverty, the wreck of high hopes, and the wintry chill of unsuccessful age. There the grass will grow green and the birds will sing above him, in a peace that his lifetime never knew.

That lifetime comprised a period of fifty-eight years. Jamieson was born in Varick street, New York, in 1810. His mother was an American lady, of remarkable talents, and from her he inherited his extraordinary skill in mimetic art. His father was an Irish Protestant, a man of strong individuality and notable independence of character — qualities that reappeared in his son. The boy was taught to read and to write, and that was all ; yet in mature life he was a man of liberal culture, and as a Shakespeare scholar he held a high rank. At an early age he was apprenticed to a lapidary and in that art he acquired facility. His cameos were models of artistic beauty and truth. In early manhood he went to Washington, where he made many excellent cameo portraits — of Henry Clay and of other distinguished men — and where he became a favourite, both as a gentleman and an artist. His taste and desire, however, impelled him toward the stage, and for that profession he studied and practised assiduously in several amateur dramatic societies. His first regular professional appearance was made at the Bowery theatre, under the management of Hamblin, in 1835, in his own farce, *The Chameleon*. His success was good and he remained an actor all his days. He was engaged at the National theatre, in Church street, New York, in 1839; he appeared in Philadelphia for the first time on October 9, 1840; and he made a professional visit to England in 1861. At one time he played opposite parts to the elder Booth and to Edwin Forrest. His Iago was his best Shakespearean impersonation, although he also played Othello well, and he was a superb reader of Hamlet. But he did not make a name as a Shakespearean actor. In later years he played "character" parts, such as Pete in *The Octoroon*, and Steve Hargrave, the Softy, in *Aurora Floyd*. The latter performance was given at Niblo's theatre, in April 1863, and was greeted with critical and popular applause, as a faithful and harrowing portrait of a semi-idiotic wretch.

In November of the same year Jamieson played an engagement at the Olympic, where two of his dramas were produced — *There's No Such Word As Fail*, and *As you Sow, you must Reap*. The former is a neatly finished and wittily written piece, and the author played in it with vivacity and refinement as an Irish gentleman. In *As you Sow* he played Moses Mole, a detective officer. That drama did not succeed. It contains one strong character, — Dr. Deadly Nightshade, — in which James H. Stoddart made a hit. So closed Jamieson's last engagement in New York. He married Miss Caroline Elwood, an actress.

His last professional appearance was made in Yonkers, where he resided for several years and was highly esteemed, and where he met with an awful fate. The express train on the Hudson River railroad that left New York at its usual hour on Saturday night, October 3, bore with it his death. He had gone up on an earlier train and been carried beyond the Yonkers station and landed at Glenwood, whence he walked back on the railway line. The express met him when he was within a few hundred yards of safety. He was instantly killed. He could not have known a moment of pain. But it is inexpressibly sad to think that a man so gifted, who had suffered so much, should have perished in such a way. Overhead the stars shone faintly down. Near by flowed the noble river. He was alone with the darkness and with his thoughts. He was already marked off from among the living. It may be hoped that, in those solemn moments, he forgave his enemies, as they must now forgive him. To one shadow that was cast upon his life, and that did him great harm, — his alleged complicity with the domestic troubles of Edwin Forrest, — a passing allusion will suffice. He spoke of it to me, and declared himself innocent; and innocent I believe him to have been. No kinder heart remains. He had faults, and they marred his character and hurt his fortunes. He had great pride of intellect; his convictions were rigid; he was not free from passionate prejudice; his impetuous irritability sometimes perplexed his judgment; his independence of character was incapable of policy; he often told the truth at the wrong time; he espoused unpopular doctrines if they happened to suit his humour; he was emphatically a man for the few and not the many. He

attained local eminence and he lived to
see it slip from his grasp and to find himself greatly misunderstood, and he became
embittered. But there were hours when
the clouds lifted and the fine genius found
ample play in the happy intercourse of
social life. To acknowledge that fine genius — to say that it existed and has passed
away — is the purpose of these few words
of remembrance. In the tumult of active
life the great world will rush onward past
his memory, as the fatal train rushed onward past his lifeless body; but there is
time to cast a flower of love and pity on
his grave.

IX.

LIFE AND GENIUS OF CUSHMAN.

1815 — 1876.

THERE is something so awfully impressive in the vanishing of a great genius and a great force of noble intellect and character out of the world that reverence must pause before the spectacle, no less in humility than in sorrow. The historian of our time will review many important and significant lives, and will lay the laurel upon many a storied tomb; but he will honour no genius more stately or more singular than that which sleeps in the coffin of Charlotte Cushman. It is difficult if not impossible to do justice to such a life. The end, which came February 18, 1876, in Boston, though not unexpected, was sudden; and it came upon the mind with a solemn force, — prompting to silent thought and fond remembrance more than to words.

Charlotte Cushman was a member of one

of the original Puritan families. Her first
ancestor in America, Robert Cushman, a
minister, came over with the Pilgrims to
New England. Her father was a merchant
of Boston, and she was born in Richmond
street, in that city, — being the eldest of
five children, — on July 23, 1815. Her
mother's name was Saunders, and Saunders
was her own middle name, though she did
not habitually use it. Her birthplace was
next door to that of John Gilbert, the comedian, and they played together as children.
A schoolhouse bearing the name of Cushman now stands on the site of those build-
ings. Charlotte's father died while she was
yet a young girl, and left his family in poverty ; and that bereavement was ultimately
the means of embarking her upon a public
career. Her first appearance occurred at
a concert in Boston, on March 25, 1830 ; at
which time she made a good impression and
was fortunate enough to attract the notice
of a generous patron, who subsequently paid
the expenses of giving her a thorough musical education. On April 8, 1835, she came
out at the Tremont theatre as the Countess
Almaviva in *The Marriage of Figaro.*
That may be called her first regular professional appearance, and her career upon the

stage, accordingly, extended over a period of a little more than forty years.

Miss Cushman's advent was made during an engagement, at the Tremont theatre, of Mrs. Maeder (Clara Fisher), then in the enjoyment of her fresh laurels, and in days made brilliant and memorable in the history of the American theatre by the presence of Cooper, Booth, Addams, Sheridan Knowles, Dowton, Charles and Fanny Kemble, Celeste, Mary Duff, Emma Wheatley, and Ellen Tree. The second character assumed by Miss Cushman was Lucy Bertram in *Guy Mannering*. Her success was immediate and decisive, and Mr. and Mrs. Maeder presently secured for her an engagement to sing in New Orleans. There, however, —whether because of some malign influence of the climate or in consequence of an effort that she made to change her voice, —she totally lost the capacity to sing, and so ended her experience as a vocalist. That disaster made her an actress. J. H. Barton, an English tragedian, then acting in New Orleans, advised her to act, and gave her instruction ; and at length, on the night of that actor's benefit, she appeared as Lady Macbeth, and so began her dramatic career.

The performance of Lady Macbeth aroused in New Orleans much public interest and even enthusiasm, and with the prestige of that success Miss Cushman returned to the North and sought an engagement in New York. Hamblin gave her an opening at the Bowery, and her first appearance was effected there. That portion of her life was much fretted with various kinds of trouble. She had to make her way against many obstacles, and she gained no victory without hard fighting. On April 23, 1837, she appeared at the National theatre, under the management of James H. Hackett, in the character of Romeo; and it was during that engagement — namely on May 8, 1837 — that she first acted Meg Merrilies.[1] In the fall of that year she was

[1] An incorrect story with reference to Charlotte Cushman's first appearance as Meg Merrilies has been adopted and repeated in various biographies of her. It states that her first appearance as Meg Merrilies was made when the English tenor, Braham, was starring in New York. That was at the Park theatre in 1840–41. The fact is that *Guy Mannering*, in which Meg Merrilies occurs, was not announced for performance during Mr. Braham's engagement at the Park theatre, and if the piece was played at all it must have been as a substitute for some other that had been promised. Miss Cushman, moreover, was not a member of the Park

enrolled as a member of the dramatic company at the Park theatre, where she acted many parts — notably those of Goneril, Emilia, and Gertrude, with Forrest; and

theatre company at that time, but was in Philadelphia; and if she then acted Meg Merrilies at all at the Park she must have done so as a visitor from Philadelphia, at a period when she was playing, with great success, at Burton's National theatre, in the character of The Naiad Queen. Finally, the essential fact is that Miss Cushman's first appearance as Meg Merrilies was made on May 8, 1837, several years before the date alleged in those erroneous accounts, not at the Park theatre, but at the National theatre, Italian Opera house, on the corner of Church and Leonard streets, New York. She also acted the part at the Park theatre, January 25, 1839, for Mr. Brough's benefit, the cast including the beneficiary as Col. Mannering, little Jones as Henry Bertram, Morley as Gabriel, Peter Richings as Dirck Hatteraick, Mrs. Bailey as Julia Mannering, and Mrs. Richardson — Elizabeth Jefferson — as Lucy Bertram. At several later dates in that season *Guy Mannering* was announced, with Mr. and Mrs. Martyn, Miss Poole, Manvers, and Giubilei in the cast; and, as Miss Cushman remained a member of the Park company, she doubtless repeated her performance of Meg Merrilies. That was some time before Braham's début in New York, and consequently the romantic yarn respecting his experience of her acting [that he was almost paralysed by her terrific aspect] is unfounded. Miss Cushman's Meg Merrilies attracted no considerable attention in America, comparatively speaking, until after her return from her first visit to Europe.

where she made a remarkable hit as Nancy, in *Oliver Twist*. From that house she went to Philadelphia, where, for a time, she was the manager of the Walnut-street theatre. In 1844, when Macready came for the second time to the Park, she was engaged, at his earnest request, to coöperate with him ; and her success at that time was such as materially enhanced her reputation. It led, also, to one of the most important steps of her life, since it inspired her with the resolve to win repute on the English stage.

Miss Cushman went to London in 1845. Forrest was acting at the Princess's theatre, and an opportunity was obtained of effecting her appearance there. She made the plunge as Bianca, in *Fazio ;* and though coldly received during the first two acts, she aroused, in act third, unequivocal enthusiasm. The personation was, in fact, a splendid triumph of mind and fire, and Miss Cushman was at once acknowledged as an actress who, in a certain class of characters, had no superior in England. Her engagement at the Princess's theatre was continued through eighty-four nights, and she afterward made the British provincial tour with extraordinary success. In 1850 she returned to America, and was thereafter seen in many cities by great assemblages of admiring spectators. In New York she appeared at Brougham's Lyceum, at the Astor-place opera house, and at the old Broadway theatre. Her fame and her fortune had now been made, and on May 15, 1852, at the Broadway, she received a benefit and took a formal farewell of the American stage. Her second visit to England ensued; and upon her return she reappeared in New York, at Burton's new theatre, as Bianca, and afterward made a tour of the provinces. That period of professional exertion lasted from September 28, 1857, to July 6, 1858, when she again took leave of the American public. It was during this engagement that she first enacted Cardinal Wolsey, giving an embodiment which was ranked with the best impersonations of Shakespearean character.

It is not difficult to understand — remembering that Miss Cushman was a woman of weird genius, sombre imagination, great sensibility, and celibate condition; that she had been victorious by force rather than by sweetness; that for her conscientious mind and nervous organisation the practice of the dramatic art was terribly earnest; and that frequently she

was the victim of disease — in what way
she often came to believe that the limit of
her labour was reached ; that the end of her
life was near, and that her retirement from
the public view was needful. With natures
that see widely and feel deeply, such de-
spondent views of personal destiny and
worldly affairs are not unusual. Thackeray,
long before he wrote *The Newcomes*, said
of himself that his work was done and he
should accomplish no more. In the several farewells that she took of the stage
Miss Cushman acted like a woman, and
precisely like the woman that she was ;
and the censors who misjudged her upon
that point did so because they failed to
consider the probable effect on conduct of
that element of feminine weakness — that
unsatisfied, and therefore forlorn, tenderness of woman's heart, which was the core
of her rugged, stalwart nature. All of her
farewells were sincere. None of them, till
death, was final or possible.

In the autumn of 1860 Miss Cushman
was again acting in New York. She came
forward on October 1, at the Winter Garden, and she remained forty-eight nights.
In February and March 1861 she filled
another engagement at the same theatre,

and then was once more seen as Nancy in *Oliver Twist*. In June of that year she said good-bye, at New Haven, and in July she went to Europe. Her residence was established in Rome, where she gathered around herself a delightful society of artistic persons, and where she remained during the greater part of the ensuing ten years. Her love of country was ardent; and that emotion, during the dark days of the civil war, was strongly aroused. Once she came home to help the cause of the Union, and by a series of professional appearances, made in New York, Philadelphia, Boston, Baltimore, and Washington, earned nearly $10,000 for the Sanitary Commission. In 1869 her health was first impaired by encroachments of the disease which at last proved fatal. In 1870 her life was seriously imperilled, and it was thought that she would die. The indomitable spirit prevailed, however, and in 1871 she returned to the United States and resumed her public vocation, appearing as a reader of Shakespeare. In that department she had no rival, excepting Fanny Kemble; and in simplicity, imaginative weirdness, personal magnetism, humour, and stalwart force of execution her readings have not been equalled.

On September 25, 1871, Miss Cushman
acted in Booth's theatre as Queen Katharine, in *Henry VIII*. — William Creswick
personating Wolsey ; and in the course of
the engagement then begun, which lasted
till November 4, she also represented Lady
Macbeth and Meg Merrilies. Those parts,
together with Bianca, Emilia, Elvira, Helen
McGregor, and Nancy, revealed her genius
upon all of its sides. Her New York engagement was succeeded by a few others in other
cities of the Union. Then for a time she was
but seldom seen, and only as a reader. The
beautiful readings that she gave at Steinway
hall, New York, in March, 1873, and again at
the Academy of Music, in January, February, and April, 1874, will long dwell in the
recollection of many who had the privilege
and the happiness to hear them. Much
public excitement and important literary
demonstrations accompanied and signalised,
in the autumn of 1874, her final performances on the New York stage. Those, con-
sisting of Queen Katharine, Lady Macbeth,
and Meg Merrilies, were given at Booth's
theatre, between October 19 and November 7. Her last embodiment there — that
of Lady Macbeth, presented on the latter
date — was seen by a vast assemblage ; and

after it was ended an ode by R. H. Stod-
dard, an address by W. C. Bryant, a laurel
crown, the plaudits of the multitude, and
the tears of proud and saddened friendship
were commingled in farewell homage to the
queen who then and there laid down her
sceptre and departed from her throne.

A few subsequent appearances closed her
dramatic career. The most important of
those was made in Boston, at the Globe
theatre, on May 15, 1875, as Lady Macbeth,
when she was the recipient of public homage
in that city, and when she tenderly took
leave of her native and favourite community. The last months of her life were
passed at Newport, Ashfield, and Boston.
Toward the end she had recourse to a Boston chemist, who inspired her indomitable
mind with renewed hopes of recovery.
Only twenty days before her death, at the
Parker House, in Boston, she spoke to me
with cheerful confidence of her anticipated
restoration to health.[1] Her eyes were bright;

[1] The immediate cause of Charlotte Cushman's
death was pneumonia. On Saturday, February 12,
she went out from the Parker House and took a
short walk, and she then caught cold. Pneumonia
ensued, and her system, long enfeebled by cancer,
proved unable to resist that new enemy. She was
quite cheerful up to the 17th, but a change took place

her voice was firm, — though suffused in
every tone with an unconscious sadness
deeply touching and quite indescribable, —
and her noble head and reverend face indicated such a vitality as it seemed impossible that death could conquer. To the last
she was an image of majesty. The pain
that consumed her suffering body could
not quell her royal spirit. She could
look back upon a good life ; she was sustained by religious faith ; she felt upon her
gray hair the spotless crown of honour ;
she met death, as she had met life, a victor ;
and she passed from the world with all the
radiance of her glory about her — like sun-
set from a mountain peak, that vanishes at
once into the heavens.

The greatness of Charlotte Cushman was
that of an exceptional because grand and
striking personality, combined with extraor-

about 2 o'clock on that morning ; at 7 she lost
consciousness, and at ten minutes past 9 she died.
It is known that the subject of death had been in
her thoughts ; yet she fully expected to recover.
As lately as February 13 she addressed a note to
John McCullough, in which she said : "I wanted to
ask you if next November and December were engaged at your theatre in California. I hope to be
able to get well and go there, but I cannot positively
decide till the middle of May."

dinary power to embody the highest ideals of majesty, pathos, and appalling anguish. She was not a great actress merely, but she was a great woman. She did not possess the dramatic faculty apart from other faculties, and conquer by that alone ; but, having that faculty in copious affluence she poured forth through its channel such resources of character, intellect, moral strength, soul, and personal magnetism as marked her for a genius of the first order while they made her an irresistible force in art. When she came upon the stage she filled it with the weirdness and the brilliant vitality of her presence. Every movement that she made was winningly characteristic. Her least gesture was eloquence. Her voice, which was soft or silvery or deep or mellow accordingly as emotion affected it, used now and then to tremble and partly to break, with tones that were pathetic beyond description. Those were denotements of the fiery soul that smouldered beneath her grave exterior and gave iridescence to every form of art that she embodied. Sometimes her whole being seemed to become petrified in a silent suspense more thrilling than any action — as if her imagination were suddenly enthralled by the tumult and awe of its own vast perceptions. It made no difference that, toward the last, her person became a little cumbersome, that her countenance was homely, and that some of her mannerisms were mannish. The commanding character, the authentic charm of genius, the lofty individuality — strange, weird, sweet, and fascinating — were victorious all the same.

As an actress Miss Cushman was best in tragedy, whether lurid or pathetic, and in sombre melodrama. Theatrical history will probably associate her name more intimately with Meg Merrilies than with any other character. That performance was unique. It embodied physical misery, wandering reason, delirious imagination, and the wasted tenderness of a loving but broken heart; and it was tinted with the vivid colours of romance. The method by which it was projected was peculiar in this — that it disregarded probability and addressed itself to the imaginative perception. When Meg Merrilies sprang forth in the moonlight and stood, with towering figure and extended arms, tense, rigid, terrible, yet beautiful, glaring on the form of Henry Bertram, the spectator saw a creature of the ideal world and not of earth. That con-

ception may have been in the brain of Sir
Walter Scott; it was never in his page.
Miss Cushman could give free rein to her
frenzy in that character, and that was why
she loved it and excelled in it, and was able
by means of it to reveal herself so amply
and with such fine dramatic effect. What
she thus revealed was a power of passionate
emotion as swift as the lightning and as
wild as the gale — an individuality fraught
with pathos, romance, tenderness, grandeur,
the deep knowledge of grief, and the royal
strength of endurance. Her Meg Merrilies
was not her highest work, but it was her
most startling and effective one, because it
was the sudden and brilliant illumination
of her being. In presenting the concep-
tions of Shakespeare Miss Cushman's spirit
was the same, but her method was different.
As Meg Merrilies she obeyed the law of her
own nature. As Queen Katharine, which
was her greatest personation, she obeyed
the law of the poetic ideal that encom-
passed her. In that stately, sweet, and
pathetic character, and again, though to a
less extent, in the terrible yet human character of Lady Macbeth, — both of which she
apprehended through an intellect always
clear and an imagination always adequate,

— the form and limitations prescribed by
the dominant genius of the poet were scrupulously respected. She made Shakespeare
real, but she never degraded her ideal to
the level of the actual. She knew the
heights of that wondrous intuition and potent magnetism, and she lifted herself —
and her hearers — to their grand and beautiful eminence. Her best achievements in
the illustration of Shakespeare were, accordingly, of the highest order of art. They
were at once human and poetic. They were
white marble suffused with fire. They
thrilled the heart with emotion and they
filled the imagination with a satisfying
sense of beauty, power, and completeness.
They made her illustrious. They did much
to assert the possible grandeur and beneficence of the stage and to confirm it in the
esteem of thoughtful men and women.
They remain as a rich legacy in remembrance; and they will pass into history
among the purest, highest, and most cherished works that genius has inspired and
art has accomplished to adorn an age of
culture and to elevate the human mind.

X.

WILLIAM WHEATLEY.

—1816—18—.

THE present presses hard upon the past
and the change is sadly felt as the old
favourites drop away. William Wheatley
was a brilliant and distinguished actor in
his time, and the associations that cluster
about such a renown are always those of
life and pleasure — never those of death
and darkness. When such a man is taken
the sense of loss and of the evanescence of
human things comes with keen reality to
many hearts. Wheatley's career and fame
are identified with bright recollections ; and
his death awakened many minds to the sense
of mutability and decline. The roses always fade. The lights are put out. The
music dies away. The new age supersedes
the old and neither knows it nor cares for it.

William Wheatley was a native of New
York, born December 5, 1816. He was the
son of Frederick Wheatley, once a favourite

actor in Baltimore and Philadelphia — a
member of the fine company formed by
Warren and Wood for the old Holliday-
street theatre, Baltimore. His mother, who
died in 1873, was also a proficient and
popular player. He inherited talent for
acting, together with a predilection for the
stage. His first public appearance was
made when he was a child, on October 13,
1826, at the Park theatre, as Albert, in
William Tell. That was during an engagement played by Macready, who expressed
approbation of the boy and encouraged an-
ticipation of his success. For several years
thereafter, aside from a brief tour in Macready's theatrical company, he continued
to act juvenile parts at the Park theatre.
The play of *Tom Thumb* was handsomely
presented for him by Simpson, and he made
a strong impression in the chief part. In
1833 he was at the Bowery theatre, acting
walking-gentlemen. In 1834 he returned
to the Park, and was assigned to such parts
as Laertes, Henry Moreland, Charles Courtly, Sir Thomas Clifford, Alfred Evelyn, and
Claude Melnotte. The first part in which
he attracted unusual notice there was in the
drama of *Rienzi.* It is remembered as a
fragment of personal history that he cus-

tomarily went before the curtain, in the early days of his experience at the Park theatre, and, — arrayed in a fine court dress, and doubtless with that long-rolling r for which his elocution continued ever to be remarkable, — announced the plays for the ensuing night.

In 1842 Wheatley joined the dramatic company at the Walnut, Philadelphia, appearing on September 22 in that year as Doricourt in *The Belle's Stratagem* — a character which always remained a favourite with him, and in which, as in Rover in *Wild Oats,* he delighted the public by his energetic vivacity and sunbright merriment. His success in Philadelphia was brilliant and he became a popular favourite and long continued so to be. On March 24, 1843, Wheatley took a farewell benefit at the Chestnut, Philadelphia, and retired from the stage. In 1847 he played a star engagement at the New York Park, in conjunction with his brilliant sister Emma Wheatley, afterward Mrs. James Mason. At about that time he visited Nicaragua, and it is said the first American flag ever raised there was raised by his hands — at Virgin bay, on the shore of the lake. In 1853 he became associated with John Drew in the

direction of the Arch, Philadelphia, and
there he continued to manage and act — at
first with Drew, then alone, and then with
John S. Clarke — till the spring of 1861.
In the spring of 1862, after acting at Niblo's
Garden in the Wallack-Davenport Combi-
nation, he leased that theatre, and he continued to manage it till the autumn of 1868,
when he sold his interest to Messrs. Jarrett
& Palmer and finally retired from management and from the stage.

His presentation of *The Duke's Motto*,
Bel Demonio, *The Connie Soogah*, and *Arrah-na-Pogue*, during his reign at Niblo's,
were among the best efforts of his career as
a manager. He was the first representative
in America of Henri de Legardere, and by
many judges he is remembered as the best.
He presented Edwin Booth as Bertuccio
(1864), Mrs. Lander as Letitia Hardy and
Adrienne Lecouvreur, and a series of the
most prominent stars upon the stage.
Niblo's had sunk so low as to be a circus,
just before he entered it, but, under his direction, it rose to be again a theatre of the
first class. Finally, however, Wheatley
brought out there *The Black Crook*, and
committed the house to the spectacle vein.
He sold advantageously and retired at a for-

tunate time. He then lived in retirement, enjoying the ease of a comfortable fortune. The sickness and death of his wife, in 1868, seriously affected his mind, and that event, together with the encroachments of ill health, turned his thoughts to religion. He became devout and his appearance and manners were so much affected by the solemn habit of his mind that he would have been taken for a clergyman rather than an actor. He contracted a second marriage, and his last days were passed in domestic seclusion, partly at Coney Island, where he owned an estate, and partly in New York. He died in that city, on November 3, 1876.

There is no act more solemnly responsible than the forming of a public estimate of a human being after his life has ended. We know each other in this world but very little. There is much beneath alike the faces that smile and the faces which are sad that we can never know. Wheatley, in character, was artificial — that is, he was self-conscious, studious of effect, and shallow in emotion. He was, however, amiable in temperament and bright in intellect, and, as his appearance and manners were picturesque and he possessed a fine person, a handsome face, a sonorous voice, and thorough education in the actor's art, he naturally won popularity and succeeded in professional life. His individuality was strongly self-assertive and he had both the instinct and faculty of leadership and government within his especial domain. His sense of humour was exceedingly slight, so that it exercised no control over the manifestation of his weakness or his eccentricity. His bearing was pompous, yet urbane. His elocution was stately and sometimes stilted. The parts in which he was best, because truest, were showy, romantic, and pictorial. His Captain Absolute was a perfect embodiment. He was admirable in Claude Melnotte and in Doricourt. His acting did not inspire affectionate interest and it may be doubted whether any performance that he gave is remembered by any person with delight. He acted Hamlet, Romeo, and other high parts in the drama, but he did not permanently identify his fame with any of them. His influence upon the stage was at times good, but it was neither deep, comprehensive, nor permanent. He was not a great actor and he was not so devoted to dramatic art as to seek, in his administration of theatres, for results that are higher, finer, and more ennobling than long runs and good business. Opinion will differ as to the degree of mischief he wrought by introducing *The Black Crook* upon the American stage. That piece represented a style of amusement that has intermittently prevailed in the English-speaking theatre from the days of Sir William Davenant, and Wheatley cannot be charged with having invented it. The sensual spectacle, however, is a kind of theatrical display that has done injury, and it is a subject for regret that his name was ever associated with its evil influence. The student of the history of the American theatre will pause but briefly on the life of William Wheatley. He will live as the central figure in divers groups of comic incidents, growing out of his characteristic habits of pomp, parade, and unconsciously ludicrous artifice. To the story-teller he is a legend and a boon. To the student of acting and of the growth and changes of dramatic art there is but one lesson deducible from his professional life, — that the line and extent of manifestations of ability in acting are prescribed and limited by the actor's temperament.

XI.

A SHORT LIFE OF OWENS.

1823 — 1886.

TO think of John E. Owens is to recall one of the most comical men that have graced and cheered the stage. He was both humourist and comedian. All his life he was a close student of the drama and of the art of acting, and he devotedly laboured to equip himself as an artist; nor did he fail in that endeavour — for his impersonations were diversified, and each of them was brilliantly distinct and thoroughly and finely finished. Yet Owens was more indebted to nature than to art for those characteristic attributes that made him great. The development of humour upon the stage within the last thirty years has taken the direction of crackling wit and dry drollery. The comedians of that period, with scarcely an exception, have been men of slender person, thin visage, acute mind, incisive voice, and intellectual and elaborate method. The

predominant and most approved style has
been the style of Charles Mathews. Art,
in its best representatives, has usually concealed art, and its manifestations have
often been delightful. Wallack, Murdoch,
Sothern, Boucicault, Clarke, J. K. Mortimer, Raymond, Lewis, Stoddart, Wynd-
ham, and others of that school, have given
pleasure to thousands and some of them
have gained renown. Yet all this while
scarcely one comedian has arisen in whom
the element of humour has revealed itself as
an affluent and .spontaneous force. The
essentially unctuous comic actors — Holland, Blake, Warren, Florence, Setchell,
and, above all, Owens — were the survivors
of an earlier generation — as Jefferson is,
who is unique and stands by himself. It
has been a scientific and a critical period,
and the feverish anxiety of it has every-
where manifested itself in the growth of
discontent, and in the decline of joy.
Upon the stage that anxiety has appeared
in the hardness and metallic glitter that
ensue from acrid strife and ravenously ambitious effort. The Wilks type of actor,
indeed, has had its successors, all along.
The Munden type has reappeared in Farren
and Fisher and Gilbert. There has been

no lack of intellect, or of brilliant vivacity,
or of pitiless satire, or of grotesque and
sardonic burlesque; but of happiness the
stage has given few signs. Burton, who
transmitted the tradition of Haynes, and
Suett, and Liston, and Reeve — Burton, at
the sound of whose voice every heart beat
happily and every face smiled — has had
no successor, born and reared in our time.
Owens, at the age of seventeen, was associated with Burton, then thirty-six, and
was his disciple and belonged to his period;
and Owens was the last comedian of that
happy lineage and that auspicious strain.
Even to remember him now — for those
who knew his acting, before the fever of
the age began to perplex its freedom and
chill its sunshine, as it did toward the last,
when he tried to adjust his fine powers to
such characters as Elbert Rogers in *Es-
meralda* and Hezekiah Perkins in *Cooke's
Corners* — is to be composed, refreshed, and
cheered.

Tragedy, with all its difficulties, is easier
for the actor than comedy. The tragedian
can, to some extent, depend upon his theme
for his effects. The comedian must depend
upon himself. With him, therefore, natural powers are more essential than acquired

facilities. Owens was born to be a comic
actor. He was intrinsically funny. His
personality was comical and at the same
time lovable. He was thoughtful in mind
and affectionate in heart, but above all he
was a creature of buoyant and merry temperament. He enjoyed life, absolutely and
fully, and he did not trouble himself with
fruitless and saddening speculation as to
its origin or its destiny. He could, whenever he pleased, look at practical affairs in
the light of common sense, and he could
see them precisely as they are, and could
deal with them in a perfectly practical
spirit. His character was exceedingly
strong and his principles were those of inflexible rectitude. Habitually, however, he
saw everything in its comic aspect, and
there was no trifle from which he could not
derive mirth. He was full of kindness and
of the desire to make others as happy as
himself. His humorous vitality was prodigious. It sparkled in his bright brown
eyes; it rippled in the music of his rich,
sonorous, flexible voice; it exulted in the
bounteous health of his vigorous constitution; it rejoiced in his alert demeanour, his
elastic step, his beaming smile, his exuberant and incessant glee. He was when act-

ing, too truly an artist ever to intercept
with his personality the spectator's view of
the character he had assumed; but, when
giving a humorous part, he invariably conveyed the impression of joyous ease and
personal relish. His cheeriness overflowed.
His comic acting was rosy with health and
redolent of enjoyment. He never imparted
the sense of inadequacy and of effort. His
humour — which was ludicrous drollery instinct with kindness — was diffused from
the hydrant and not from the tap. He refreshed with the excess and superfluity of
a rich nature. He was never strenuous;
never complex; never stilted. In a word,
his comic power was elemental, and the
natural manifestation of it inevitably resulted in comic effect. He could indeed
play serious parts, for he possessed a true
vein of pathos, and he lacked neither authority nor repose; but his distinctive gift
was that of comic power, and as long as he
acted from the distinctively humorous impulse he never went astray from nature,
and he never failed to touch the heart.
His embodiment of Caleb Plummer, in
which there was an exquisite strain of
spontaneous and involuntary tenderness,
was the perfection of humour, and the eyes

that smiled at it always smiled at it through love and tears. It was only in those moods when he was critical of himself, and chose to act from precept rather than from instinct, that Owens sometimes marred the beauty of his art and left his hearers unmoved. At those times he thought it essential to be what is styled "true to life," and in becoming literal and photographic he became monotonous and dry. The excess, for example, to which he sometimes carried the coarser traits of Solon Shingle was one result of that critical caprice. No dramatic embodiment was ever funnier; but it would have been just as funny, and it would have been more endearing, if it had not been quite so true. Those two impersonations, however — Caleb Plummer and Solon Shingle — marked him as a great comedian and established his rank beyond dispute or question. His regular repertory comprised about fifty parts, but those were at the head of the list, and with those were intimately associated Dr. Pangloss, in *The Heir-at-law;* Joshua Butterby, in *Victims;* Henry Dove, in *Married Life;* Grimaldi, in *The Life of an Actress;* Dr. Ollapod, in *The Poor Gentleman;* Horatio Spruggins, in *Forty Winks;* John Unit, in *Self;* Mr. Gilman,

in *The Happiest Day of My Life*; Graves,
in *Money*; Meddle, Toodle, and Paul Pry.
He was the best representative of Uriah
Heep that has been seen. He played Silky,
in *The Road to Ruin*, better than it has
ever been played on the American stage,
except, perhaps, by John Sefton. He was
equally delightful in characters so widely
contrasted as Micawber and Aminidab
Sleek, Farmer Allan, and Billy Lackaday.
He developed all the humour there is in
Touchstone, and he was the best Tony
Lumpkin of his time. He comprehended
character at a glance, and he completely
merged himself in his ideal. Each of his
embodiments was stamped with his signet
— as it ought to have been, for no man becomes an actor merely because he puts on
a successful disguise — but each of them
was a different person in every particular.
He undertook no quest of theatrical exotics,
but was content with accepted types. He
was a conservative in his profession; he
respected it and he kept it pure. His career as an actor covered a period of forty-
two years — from 1840 to 1882 — and
during the whole of that time his name
was the symbol of worthy ambition and
honourable achievement.

Owens was sometimes a member of the stock; sometimes a star; and at almost all times a manager. He managed theatres in Baltimore, New Orleans and Charleston, and he gained a large fortune. In 1853 he bought a farm, near Baltimore, and named it Aigburth Vale — in affectionate memory of the dwelling place of his ancestors, in Wales. There he built a magnificent house, and there he had a home for nearly thirty-four years, in happy companionship with his devoted wife. Owens was born at Liverpool, England, April 2, 1823, and he died at Aigburth Vale, December 7, 1886, and was buried at Greenmount Cemetery, Baltimore. It was a good life, unpretentiously devoted to good objects, adorned with good deeds, and irradiated with the sunshine of gentleness and humour. Owens was a great comedian — one of original genius and independent mind — and as you study him you are more than ever convinced that the best individual development, alike for itself and the world, is that which takes its own course and is not moulded by the influence of the time through which it passes. In private Owens was gentle, genial, sympathetic and kind, and those who were nearest to him loved him best. The story

of his career has been told by his widow
with absolute simplicity and truth.   Her
Memories manifest fine discernment of his
characteristic traits, together with sound
judgment of his acting, and they comprise
anecdotes that illustrate the quality of his
humour and the variety of his experience.
If he could know her narrative one can
well imagine that he would say, with the
poet in whom he took such deep delight, —

> " After my death I wish no other herald,
>   No other speaker of my living actions,
> To keep mine honour from corruption,
>   But such an honest chronicler as Griffith."

XII.

JEAN DAVENPORT LANDER.

JEAN DAVENPORT (Mrs. Lander) was born at Wolverhampton, in Shropshire, England, on May 3, 1829. Her father was a lawyer, but he left the bar for the stage, and became the manager of the Richmond theatre, where, at the age of eight, his daughter Jean made her first professional appearance. That was in 1837, and the character she represented was that of Little Pickle, in *The Manager's Daughter*, a piece that is also known as *The Spoiled Child*, and, in Dion Boucicault's version, as *The Young Actress*. Little Pickle was a favourite character with little Jean, and she made a hit in it, as she also did at the same time in Richard the Third. It is remembered as an interesting incident that she was the first representative of Richard seen in the Richmond theatre after Edmund Kean's death, and that she wore the Richard hat that had been owned and worn by that great actor. Immediately after that appearance she fulfilled successful engagements in several British cities, winning a special triumph at Dublin. In 1839 she came to America. Her first appearance here was made at the National theatre in Leonard street, under the management of the elder Wallack. Afterward she played star engagements in other cities. In 1842 she returned to Europe and travelled in Italy and France. Her education at that time was conducted by private tutors. In Paris she studied music under the tuition of Garcia. So signal and excellent, indeed, was the musical talent which she manifested in early life, that at one time the question was seriously debated whether she should adopt music or the drama as a profession. Choosing the latter, she thoroughly schooled herself in its rudiments, and by constant study and practice she steadily and surely rose in efficiency and in reputation. Several of the more mature successes of her youth were won at the London Olympic, after her return from America. There, in 1845, she played Shakespeare's Juliet, Julia, in *The Hunchback*, and the Countess, in *Love*, and there she became a favourite ; but serious illness compelled her to retire from the stage. On her reappearance, after some time, she received a testimonial benefit, under the auspices of the Lord Mayor of London — a significant token of well-earned popularity. In 1846 she went into Holland, taking an English company, with which she acted at Hamburg, Hanover, Amsterdam, Rotterdam, and the Hague. That tour occupied about two years and was remunerative. Indeed, the young actress appears to have aroused, in an unusual degree, the enthusiasm of the Hollanders. On her last night at Hamburg the stage was strewn with flowers. At Hanover the theatre was given her rent-free. At Amsterdam she was "commanded" to play before the king, as Julia. Returning to England in 1848, she made her appearance as a public reader. Fanny Kemble had not then entered that field, and Miss Davenport soon held a conspicuous eminence. Her first reading was given in Oxford. She embellished her Shakespearian readings, when occasion offered, by singing the incidental music. She was one of the first female artists, subsequent to the time of Mrs. Siddons, that attempted to give readings from Shakespeare. Her second visit to America was made in 1849, and so great was the professional success she achieved here that she became deeply attached to the country and determined to make it her home. Her father, who had always been her companion and manager, died at Cincinnati on July 5, 1851, and, in the following year, she went once more to England, there to settle the affairs of her parent's estate and to study for the next dramatic season. Fresh successes awaited her on her return, twelve months later, to her adopted country. In Peg Woffington, Adrienne Lecouvreur, Letitia Hardy, the Countess, and Camille she made at that time a deep impression. Her first visit to California was made in 1855. She was in England in 1856-7, and again in 1859. On October 30, 1860, at San Francisco, Jean Davenport became the wife of Frederick West Lander — then a civil engineer, and a government agent for pacificating the Indians in the far West. Her married life was happy, but it was brief. As soon as the war began her husband joined the Union army, was made a general, and lost his life in battle on March 3, 1862. He was an intrepid, noble gentleman, and has left an unsullied memory. His widow, who, at the time of her marriage, had retired from the stage, did not resume it for several years, preferring, in the meanwhile, to devote herself to the cause in which her husband's life had been sacrificed. That cause she served as an hospital nurse, in Washington, ministering to the wants of wounded and dying soldiers. In February 1865 Mrs. Lander reappeared upon the stage at Niblo's theatre, New York, in a drama entitled *Mesalliance*. The coming of Ristori brought a new set of characters into vogue — Queen Elizabeth, Mary Stuart, Marie Antoinette, etc. — and Mrs. Lander availed herself of that new predilection of popular taste. Her Queen Elizabeth was first seen at the National theatre, Washington, in April 1867. Mrs. Lander has retired from the stage, but while she remained upon it she was steadfastly faithful to the legitimate drama, honouring the art whereby she prospered and keeping alive the sacred fire.

XIII.

ADA REHAN AS ROSALIND.

IN the production of *As You Like It* that
was accomplished at Daly's Theatre on
December 17, 1889, an effort was made —
and it was attended with unequivocal success — to illustrate that beautiful comedy
in a mood of dramatic art and by scenic
embellishments harmonious with its spirit
of vernal bloom. Every tone and every
tint of melancholy was rigorously excluded,
equally from the performance and from the
picture. The old theory, which mingled
pensive sadness with buoyant gayety in the
interpretation of that piece was abandoned.
That theory is based in part upon the fact
that the theme of the comedy is life in
exile ; in part upon Orlando's allusion to
" the shade of melancholy boughs " ; in
part upon the mournful cadence of " Blow,
blow, thou winter wind " ; in part upon the
presumption that the prominent figure of
Jaques is a sort of pastoral Hamlet ; and
in part upon an ultra-poetical estimate of

the character of Rosalind. Those denotements, considered apart from the context, naturally prompt the studious mind to a sombre view of Shakespeare's design; and in accordance with that view it has commonly been maintained that, with all its glittering vitality, *As You Like It* is a mournful play. Yet, in fact, the piece neither contains a sad person nor anywhere supplies a current of sad thought. The exiles are as merry as gypsies. Orlando is only hungry when he remarks upon the "melancholy boughs." The plaintive sigh of the winter wind is but a stray note of regret, much intensified by Dr. Arne's delicious but sorrowful music. Jaques is in no sense a Hamlet, for not only he does not suffer, but he takes a keen delight in his contemplative rumination and in his faculty of cynical satire. And Rosalind, while absolutely pure and entirely sweet and lovely, is a creature of flesh and blood, neither made of the clouds nor resident in them, and bent upon enjoying, within the limit of right conduct, whatever animal as well as sentimental comfort there is to be enjoyed in her earthly state. In one word, the atmosphere of the comedy is happiness; nor is that fact invalidated by the consideration that Shakespeare's mood, when he wrote it, was tinged with a gravity of thought which, while humorous, did not cease to be severe.

All strong minds are intrinsically grave. All men who see human life deeply and widely, however much they may smile and banter over it, perceive in it much that is painful and sad. Shakespeare, who was more than thirty-five years old when *As You Like It* was written, had "gained his experience"; and it is distinctly obvious, in the characters of Jaques and Touchstone, and in the words of the First Lord and the Banished Duke, that life for him had lost its illusions, and that while he could treat it with playful toleration and satirical pleasantry, he saw its trouble and its pathos, — that taint of evil in human nature which has made and which will perpetuate the warp in human affairs, and which renders invariable and long-continued happiness impossible to man. But the freedom and grace of the composition and the delicate exaggeration to which character, conduct, and events are subjected in it show that it was spontaneously made, with a sweetly humorous drift, and with the intention to create, in its picture of life, an effect of quizzical merriment. The name of the piece is eloquent of its intention. You are to accept it as it may strike your fancy, whether grave or gay, philosophical or careless, profound or superficial, ardent or cold. Shakespeare could be strenuous when he chose to be; but in *As You Like It* he quizzes and banters, he dreams and drifts, he clothes everything in motley; and in so far as he supplies any incentive that is direct he bids us to "fleet the time carelessly, as they did in the golden world." He took a romance of his day and he turned it into a comedy. He took it because he saw in the theme — which is a love-story in the woods — an opportunity to reflect unusually charming and quaint aspects of nature in the rosy mirror of pure poetic art. He transfigured it; he embellished it; he introduced into it new material and new characters (Jaques, Touchstone, Martext and Audrey); he suffused the structure with the radiance of his illimitable imagination and his affluent and beautiful style; and he sent his work into the world to be a perpetual fountain of pleasure. Since it is a happy piece, therefore, the investiture of it ought to be joyous. That view was taken by Augustin Daly, and in his practical application of that view he achieved the brightest, gayest,

loveliest production of *As You Like It* that
our stage has known. The scenery made
you think of Browning's glowing aspiration, "Oh, to be in England, now that
April's there!" Even the time of the antique incidental music was quickened to
harmonise with the abounding and rejuve-
nating spirit that controlled in the representation, — the spirit of bud and blossom
and velvet verdure, golden sunshine, fra-
grant breezes, and ecstatic human vitality.

Of those symbols, and of the soul which
they denote, Rosalind is the exquisite personification, and therefore in a manifest
sense Rosalind is the comedy ; and when
the comedy is acted, the representative of
Rosalind must necessarily stand forth as
the most conspicuous and important figure
in the picture. Shakespeare is not laughing
in his portraiture of that delightful and enchanting woman. She was, in his imagination, intended to be spiritually pure,
intellectually brilliant, physically handsome, lithe, ardent, and tender, — the incarnation of glowing health, bewitching
sensibility, passionate temperament, and
captivating personal charm. Her distinctive superficial attribute is piquant sprightliness, but beneath that she has a deep heart,

and the freedom of her conduct and the
exuberance of her wit flow out of her absolute sincerity and innocence. She has not
the half-mournful sweetness of Viola, nor
the self-centred, stately composure of Portia, nor the tragic intensity of Imogen : she
is just the type of a healthful, happy, sparkling woman, predominant by rich, pure,
and charming personality, loving dearly and
wishful to be loved, and ultimately exultant
in the ecstatic consciousness that her natural wish has accomplished its aim. There
are persons who appear to resent that they
possess bodies, and there are many who
seem ashamed of their emotions. Not so
with Rosalind. She is exultant in her
physical life, her heart is full of tenderness,
and what her heart feels her tongue must
speak.

That way the character was apprehended
by Ada Rehan, and that way — acting it
for the first time in her life — she embodied
it, charming every observer by the copious
and prodigal exuberance of her sweetness
and her brilliancy, and winning the honour
that is due to royal achievement in dramatic art. The three dramatic conditions
of Rosalind — the woman, the woman playing the boy, and the boy playing the

woman — could not be more perfectly dis-
criminated than they were by her, and
throughout them all the soft refinement of
the personality was never for an instant
frayed or warped by even the least tone of
that involuntary coarseness which, under
such conditions, excitement is sure to develop in a vulgar nature. The innate
delicacy of Miss Rehan's embodiment of
Rosalind was the principal ingredient of
its alluring captivation. The spectator
of her modest perplexity on the score of
doublet and hose felt that his spirit was
brought into contact with a nature radically good, — a nature of which noble sincerity was a cardinal virtue and to which
meanness was impossible. Furthermore,
that delicacy was found to be perfectly
compatible with brilliant and incessant
sprightliness. Throughout the first act,
which passes at court, Miss Rehan made
Rosalind interesting by simple loveliness
and by a bearing that was invested more
with the superiority of genius or of original
character than with the distinction of royal
manner. Yet that distinction was not
omitted. Her personal fitness for the part
was proved in nobility of stature and presence, in opulence of essentially feminine

charms, and in sympathetic voice and limpid melody of speech. The act was not
used merely as a preparation for getting
into male attire. There was ample revelation in it of the sweetness, the passion, and
the buoyancy of Rosalind's nature, and
Miss Rehan gave a touching expression of
the bewildered tremor naturally incident
to the first love of a girl's heart. That was
in the scene of the wrestling. Later, when
Rosalind emerges in her state of liberty and
not of banishment in the forest of Arden,
Miss Rehan's gleeful animal spirits soon
began to irradiate the performance, and
from that time onward the inspiriting glow
of happy-hearted raillery never flagged.
The relief that Rosalind experiences as
soon as she knows that she is beloved by
Orlando, liberates her into a gentle frenzy
of pleasure, and that condition is expressed
in Shakespeare by incessant frolic. In
order, however, that the mood may not become monotonous or insipid, Rosalind is
implicated in the episode of Silvius and
Phebe, which is a case of unreciprocal passion, while still another phase of the universal susceptibility is provided in the
betrothal of Touchstone and Audrey. Miss
Rehan is one of the most radically natural

performers that have appeared in our time. No one acts a poetic part with more flexibility; no one speaks blank verse with more of the fluency of a natural utterance; no one delivers prose with a nicer perception of the melody inherent in our language. It is not easy to perceive by what principle Shakespeare was governed in making those alternations of prose with verse that constitute the text of *As You Like It;* but of Rosalind's words, as they were delivered by Miss Rehan, it is true — and it was delightful — that they lapsed into one uniform current of melody, so that no listener remembered that the text is composite. Throughout Rosalind's scenes with Orlando the variety of her limpid elocution, combined with incessant animation of capricious demeanour, sustained the impersonation in a clear light of sparkling piquancy. In Rosalind's rebuke of Phebe — whose subsequent speech to Silvius is such an ample and delicious description of her person — the jocular humour and bubbling glee of the actress reached their height; and when she spoke the epilogue, which she did with zest and finish that gave point and glitter to that inadequate tag, she had vindicated her rank among the great comedians of the century.

Mr. Daly's stage version of *As You Like It*, restores to the First Lord — as that of Macready did — the speeches descriptive of Jaques, which ordinarily Jaques himself is allowed to speak. It also restores the two Pages and the song that they sing for Touchstone. It retains many scattered passages of the original text. It ends Act II. with the song of the winter wind, instead of ending it with a bit of spoken rhyme. It includes all the music that the author intended should be used. It excludes every touch of coarseness. It rejects the interpolation of *The Cuckoo Song* (from *All's Well,*) which was put into the mouth of the stage Rosalind, in Garrick's time, in order, apparently, to degrade her. (Mrs. Dancer was the first Rosalind that sang it, in 1767, at Drury Lane.) It preserves every speaking part in the original piece (there are twenty-five of them), except Sir Oliver Martext and the Second Lord. It makes a felicitous re-arrangement of incidents in the fifth act. It makes various dexterous emendations, — like that, for example, which gives "with bills on their necks" to Le Beau instead of Rosalind, and it abounds with fresh business. It requires two scenes for the first act and the beginning of the second, and thereafter several woodland scenes; and those were painted in spring-time tints, and composed with both the instinct and the remembrance of that peculiar rustic beauty which is more deliciously gentle in England than anywhere else on earth. The scene was laid, as usual, in France, to which country the text contains one implicatory allusion,[1] in the reign of Charles VIII.; but *As You Like It* passes in the dream-land of the imagination, and the Forest of Arden that Shakespeare meant, in so far as he meant an actual place, was the Forest of Arden in Warwickshire. And by a skilful blending of set pieces with panorama, the effect was secured of boundless extent and opulent luxuriance in the breezy clearings and sun-dappled glades of the fanciful forest of Arden.

With the exception of Lady Macbeth no woman in Shakespeare is so much in controversy as Rosalind. The character is thought to be almost unattainable. An ideal that is lofty, but at the same time is vague, seems to possess the Shakespeare scholar, accompanied by the pro-

---

[1] Oliver, speaking to the Wrestler says, "I'll tell thee, Charles, — it is the stubbornest young fellow of France." — *As You Like It*, Act I., Scene I.

found conviction that it never can be
fulfilled. Only a few actresses have obtained recognition as Rosalind, — chief
among them being Mrs. Pritchard, Peg
Woffington, Mrs. Dancer, Dora Jordan,
Louisa Nesbitt, Helen Faucit, Ellen Tree,
Adelaide Neilson, Mrs. Scott-Siddons, and
Miss Mary Anderson. There are obvious
difficulties in the way of giving a fine performance of Rosalind ; and yet the character is not obscure. Shakespeare built
the comedy of *As You Like It* upon the
basis of a romance, partly in prose and
partly in verse, by his contemporary,
Thomas Lodge (it was published in 1592,
dedicated to the Lord of Hudson), called
Rosalynde: Euphues' Golden Legacy.
That story of a wild girl frolicking in the
woods suggested to his imagination the
image of the unconventional woman whom
free-minded men adore. It is in Celia, and
not in Rosalind, that Shakespeare has, according to the text of the original, given
the slightly carnal touch of physical exuberance. She is fine, but she is not of the
fine strain of Rosalind. When Garrick
revived the piece she was cast to Kitty
Clive, whose strong point was not sentiment. Celia combines force, mischief, and

animal piquancy. The charm of Rosalind
is her gypsy charm. She is young, handsome, pure, merry, and noble; and beneath a sparkling outside of nimble wit,
smiling levity, and amiably satirical banter
she veils a passionate temperament, sensitive to every fine impulse and every lovely
influence. The reason why she is not more
often embodied in a competent and enthrall-
ing manner is that her enchanting quality
is something that cannot be assumed, — it
must be possessed; it must exist in the
fibre of the individual, and its expression
will then be spontaneous. Art can accomplish much, but it cannot supply the inherent captivation that constitutes the
puissance of Rosalind. Miss Rehan possesses that quality, and the method of her
art was the fluent method of natural grace.
She did not try to be anything more than a
woman. She did not grope after abstract
meanings. She dashed into the woodland
frolic in a mood of gleeful happiness; and
the image of a buoyant womanhood that
she embodied was sweetly reckless, because
absolutely innocent as well as ardently
impetuous. The performance was marked
by incessant movement and sparkle, and
yet it did not become monotonous or insin-

cere, because it was continuously fraught with suggestiveness of the pure, simple, happy, and bounteous nature beneath it. Those courtship passages in the forest, wherein the boy plays the woman, drag wearily when Rosalind is not the actual woman of Shakespeare's dream. In Miss Rehan's portrayal they ran with the sparkle of the brook in spring-time. Her spirit was in the personation, and her spirit brims over with its affluence equally of feeling and of frolic. Rosalind is not one of the cold, experimental women who stop short with wishing, not to love, but to experiment by making men love them; she is herself a lover, and the crowning ecstasy of her life arrives in that golden hour when at length she is sure of Orlando's fidelity. Few emotions that women feel are of a more sacred character than the one that must be experienced and conveyed by the representatives of Shakespeare's favourite heroine. Miss Rehan rose naturally to the height of the character and sustained herself easily at that poise.

The omission of Mrs. Gilbert from the cast of *As You Like It*, while much regretted, was unavoidable, there being no part for her in the comedy; but the image of that exquisite and admirable actress — the unmatched interpreter of eccentricity, whether serious or comic, in elderly women — will long abide in memory, and will always stand, in the historical record, as intimately and tenderly associated with the professional triumphs of Ada Rehan. And as often as the name of Mrs. Gilbert is remembered, it will also be remembered that no actress of her time surpassed her in kindness of heart or gentleness of manner, the practical goodness that she exemplified, or the affection that she inspired. There is an element equally of pathos and of beauty in the companionship of youthful genius with ancient service and laurelled age, — a companionship that has been sweetly and touchingly illustrated in Miss Rehan's association with Mrs. Gilbert. In the relations of mimic life, Miss Rehan and Mrs. Gilbert have turned many a lovely ideal to the favour of a still lovelier reality. Those living pictures are become a memory now, growing always more precious and more sacred as we descend into the twilight, —

> "Where Past and Present, bound in one,
>   Do make a garland for the heart."

XIV.

CLARA MORRIS IN SEVERAL CHARACTERS.

THE NEW MAGDALEN is a tempting story for stage treatment, and Miss Clara Morris, in reverting to it, obeyed a natural impulse. The piece that she presented was an alteration of the one by Wilkie Collins himself, in which the intellectual power, magnetic spirit, and delicate, artistic style of Miss Ada Cavendish enabled that actress to win a brilliant success. Miss Clara Morris made changes in the text but not in the plan. There was no need of a change in either — the workmanship of Wilkie Collins, whether literary or dramatic, being excellent ; and there is no literary man of the age who would presume to meddle with any work of art once perfected by that great writer. Miss Morris retained all the dramatic points of the original play. The first act was an epitome of the exciting, pictorial, effective prologue to the novel, in which Grace Roseberry and Mercy Merrick first meet, on a battle field, and Grace Rose-

berry is struck down by a stray shot, and
Mercy Merrick takes the place of what she
supposes to be a dead woman. The second
act was a condensed exposition of subsequent events, in the English conventional
home of Lady Janet Roy. It included the
betrothal of the fictitious Grace Roseberry
to Horace Holmcroft, her meeting with
Julian Gray, and her discomfiture at the
apparition of the woman whose name and
place she had wrongfully assumed. The
third act contained the scene of the encounter between the two women, in which
the scorn and cruelty of vindictive virtue
embitter and harden the repentant soul of
vice and misfortune, and it ended with the
real Mercy Merrick's heroic act of self-conquest. The last scene was a tableau of
restitution, with such action as is designed
to urge that there may be a perfect redemption, social as well as moral, for the outcast
who repents, reforms, and has the courage
to do right. The clearly-drawn and well-
contrasted characters, the steadily acceler-
ated movement, the cumulative interest,
and the trenchant purpose of the original
story were thus distinctly presented. The
piece, indeed, did not — and no dramatic
treatment could — reproduce that fine analy-

sis of motives and that complex tissue of
sentiment, feeling, reasoning, manners, epi-
gram, and dry humour for which the novel
is remarkable.

In *The Woman in White* and *Armadale*,
which are his best novels, the mind of
Wilkie Collins seems to have been swayed
almost exclusively by his imagination. In
No Name, *Man and Wife*, *The New Magdalen*, and *The Black Robe* he manifested
a desire to connect his writings with practical questions of the age, and to enforce
moral lessons of immediate and applicable
significance. There is nowhere extant a
more subtle and cogent treatment of the
muscular development craze of the present
day than may be found in his novel of *Man
and Wife*. In that effort, and in kindred
efforts, the purpose is a moral one. *The
New Magdalen* is a plea for women who
come out of a life of vice and try to lead a
life of virtue. It is impossible, accordingly,
to restrict the discussion of the work —
whether play or novel — to its dramatic
values alone. It is a sermon as well as a
drama, and its moral values have also to
be considered. They are not clear. The
charity, the tender compassion, the human
spirit, and the hopeful and cheering drift

of the piece are obvious and unmistakable. Literature presents no instance of a better friend to woman than Wilkie Collins. In depicting Magdalen Vanstone, Rosanna Spearman, Hester Dethridge, Mercy Merrick, and Miss Gwilt, he has shown not only a profound knowledge of female human nature, but a noble and lovely sympathy with the feminine heart and temperament, and a broad, manly, lenient, and intelligent judgment as to the circumstances under which woman plays her part in the world. His spirit is even finer than that of Steele, while his wisdom is commensurate with that of Thackeray. But, in the logic of morality, which applies to Mercy Merrick, his teaching seems indefinite, for the reason that she is an exceptional woman, and therefore not a representative of the class of women to be redeemed. It was right that Sir Patrick Lundy should marry Anne Sylvester, notwithstanding he is aware that she has been betrayed under promise of marriage. Peculiar circumstances justify unusual conduct. It may be right and noble that Julian Gray should marry Mercy Merrick, who has cast her sin away, and expiated her wrong-doing by an act of moral heroism such as proves her to be innately good and supremely true. But there again the circumstances are peculiar. If every repentant sinner, man or woman, were an heroic being, it might be possible to formulate, upon such a case as that of Mercy Merrick, the principles that ought to govern society in its treatment of persons reclaimed from a vicious life. But, as things really are, the question is one that must be left to individual judgment. Furthermore, in one aspect of the subject, neither the individual nor the world can avail to regenerate the soul that has once drifted into sin. Every wound leaves its scar. Mercy Merrick is not the only human creature who cries out, in the bitterness of despair, "I can't get back!" No remorse, no repentance, no atonement will again make white and pure the spirit that sin has polluted. Wilkie Collins himself has enforced that truth, in what he makes Rosanna Spearman say, to old Betteridge, in *The Moonstone,* — "The stain is taken off, but the place shows."

Miss Morris, early in her career, indicated a proclivity for such dramatic types as involve the tumultuous passions, the shipwrecks of the heart, and the painful moral problems that are suggested in plays of the order of *The New Magdalen*. Her impersonation of Mercy Merrick was full of her passionate individuality, hysterical sensibility, and nervous force, and, in fact, was more a revelation of personal attributes than an assumption of character. In the strong scene of the third act she made a sudden and startling dramatic transition from the humility of grief to the icy composure of supercilious indifference and bland contempt, when brought to bay by Grace Roseberry, and that, and her wild intervention, to rescue and shield her enemy, were the splendid points and peculiar features of her performance. The earnest warmth of a woman's heart, tortured and struggling, was felt likewise throughout the art. The light, household manner into which it pleased Miss Morris periodically to lapse was not that of the character, but of herself. The art structure of the performance was perplexed by aimless wanderings across the scene and much impulsive posturing and gesticulation, which had an angular effect, as of a person acting at haphazard and taking the chance of somehow coming out right. Miss Morris's dramatic art, indeed, sometimes suggested Lord Timothy Dexter's autobiography, in which the punctuation marks, of all sorts, are printed at the end of the book, — the reader being invited to scatter them through the text in whatsoever manner may please him best. Yet every one of her performances presented superb points.

The personation of *Miss Multon* was, of its kind, a great work, and one that exerted an extraordinary influence. The play of *Miss Multon* is an adapted translation of a French piece which was built on the basis of the English play on the subject of Mrs. Henry Wood's novel of *East Lynne*. The new version is superior to the old one — being round, compact, pointed, smoothly written, swiftly impelled by natural incidents, and made exciting and affecting by a series of situations, each stronger than its predecessor. A fine point of its superiority, moreover, resides in the skill with which it veils the ruinous misdeed of its heroine, and so directs the attention of the spectator rather upon the consequences of sin than upon the evil and reprehensible misconduct which has made punishment inevitable, salutary, and just. The dramatist comes at once to Hecuba, and presents the image of a miserable, repentant woman, who, having fled from husband, children, and home, is urged, by contrition and by strong maternal instinct, to return thither in disguise, and to accept a position of servitude, where once she had filled the throne of sovereignty. The first two acts are devoted to a statement of the relations of the persons implicated in the plot. The last three acts exhibit the experience of the unfortunate and wretched woman, when thus established in the household of the man whom she has wronged, and who, supposing her to be dead, has married again. An added element of power and pathos is gained by making the husband cognizant of the identity of the Miss Multon whom he has engaged as a governess for their children. The third and fourth acts of the piece amount to a vivisection of the human heart. Trial after trial, blow after blow, agony ever changing, growing and deepening — that is the burden of the action. A desperate avowal of the truth ensues and an afflicting death ends the fruitless endeavour to atone for wrong and to rebuild the shattered fabric of innocence and happiness.

The use of such a dark and hopeless subject for the purpose of a domestic play was not, perhaps, judicious. A result of more than common good should be attained, in order to justify the effect that follows upon such an accumulation of miseries. The simple moral lesson of fidelity to virtue and duty scarcely requires such harrowing enforcement as that. Those persons, however, who need a terrible warning may find it in *Miss Multon*. No voice from the pulpit ever spoke with such an effect of piteous grief and overwhelming conviction as were seen to flow from that drama.

The acting of Clara Morris in the character of the repentant wife and heartbroken mother presented the spectacle of a human being absorbed and enthralled with agony. The individuality of the actress seemed swallowed up in the identity which her imagination — acting through the heart — made real. It was a kind of acting that had no apparent laws and could be tried by no standard. The artist felt the grief that she undertook to convey, and she allowed her expression of it to follow the current of her feeling, without heed to form or to method of utterance. Having seen her several times in the character, however, the auditor would discover that in fact she followed the same general line of action upon all occasions — which means that the exciting cause being the same her nature would utter itself in the same manner. It seemed evident, though, that neither intellect nor artistic purpose had much to do with the result. The mechanism was almost chaotic. Contortions of the body, convulsions of the face, disproportionate attitudes, extravagant gestures, spasmodic starts and changes, and indescribable wild moans and cries were commingled in that wonderful embodiment with moments of sweet dignity, lovely tenderness, exalted fortitude, and an exquisitely simple expression of simple emotion. Over the whole effort there was the lawlessness of a genius that is a law to itself; and the effect of the effort was that of perfect pathos.

There are actors who feel and there are actors who do not feel, and the same results of "realism" are produced by both. Clara Morris is of the former class. There is a deep vein of rich humour in her nature and that forms its relief; but there seems to be little or no capacity of that intellectual isolation of herself from herself which would enable her at all times to modulate the expression of feeling with the absolute propriety and refinement that maintain its unbroken beauty without impairing its power. Clara Morris's exposition of the remorse that is felt by the sinner, and the torture that she suffers in living a false life under the eyes of moral resentment and indignant justice, was overwhelming in its bitter truth. The curbing of grief and of passion in the scenes of trial was accomplished with an afflicting tragic power. The expression of the strong will was intense and noble. The portraiture of the peevishness of sickness, the half imbecile tone of a wandering mind, and all the presaging denotements of mortal dissolution was wonderful in fidelity. The performance was a memorable reflex of the individuality of genius, an extraordinary dramatic achievement, and a cogent and pathetic moral lesson.

Another characteristic embodiment by Clara Morris was Esther, in *The New Leah*, written by Augustin Daly, on the basis of a translation of Dr. Mosenthal's German play of *Deborah*. The heroine of *The New Leah* is a Hebrew girl. She is loved by a Christian youth, and she loves him in return. For his sake she is willing to desert her friends, leave her people, and abandon her religion. He likewise purposes to forsake his home and kindred on account of his love. Their meetings are held by stealth, and usually at night. Their plan is to marry and depart into a foreign country. The scene of their loves and other experiences is a little village and its rustic neighbourhood in Germany. The time is summer, in the early part of the eighteenth century, — a period when, in some countries of Europe, the Jews were proscribed and persecuted. The fate of those lovers is pathetic, and it comes near being tragic. They are parted by the treacherous and malignant machinations of an apostate Jew. The youth is persuaded to believe that the maiden is false to him, and has betrayed him for money. He breaks faith with her, and he weds another woman. On their wedding day the Jewess meets him in the churchyard, and curses him for his perfidy, after which ebullition of love turned to hatred she wanders away, a homeless and destitute outcast. Years afterward she returns to the scene of her trial and anguish, meets her former lover — now a husband and father — forgives him, and, under saddest circumstances, changes her curse into a blessing. That story, dramatically told, in four acts, excites admiration for a beautiful, passionate nature, awakens sympathy with grief cruelly inflicted and in great part patiently suffered, thrills the heart with an image of frenzy, and elevates the mind with a portrayal of saint-like yet woman-like magnanimity. A drawing of the simple, rural, domestic life of a pastoral people, touched with gentle piety, homely humour, and the commonplace, forms a background to a representative tale of love and sorrow.

The heroine Esther was personated in a powerful, passionate manner by Clara Morris. Her Jewish maiden was not dazzling in ripe, dusky beauty, nor fervid and ominous in Oriental, intense self-poise; but she was mournfully lovely to the eye, and her picturesque loveliness was surcharged with passionate tenderness. She did not stir the imagination, but she appealed directly to the heart; and, in the quality of sympathy — the power to captivate the feelings, apart from the satisfaction of the sense of the ideal — she was the best representative of the part that has been seen. Miss Bateman was austere, intellectual, and fierce, and at the same time she was cold. Ristori was mature, artificial, melo-dramatic. Marie Seebach was over-spiritual. Janauschek, fiery and superb in action, was cumbrous, and over physical. Clara Morris, though she did not lift the ideal to Seebach's height, was excellent in the youth, grace, softness, and fire of the tender woman : and those attributes she welded into a form at once picturesque, mournful, and weird. She made a good effect in the defiance of the mob. She greatly excited her listeners in the curse scene — the religious element commingling with the human. In the lover's meeting, the scene of the repulse, and the tender passages at the close, she surpassed all previous representatives of the part and entirely satisfied all of its requirements. Her conquest was through the emotions. Her method was controlled by taste and made symmetrical by repose. Her best moments were those of frenzy, as when love struggles in the heart with knowledge that it is wasted and in vain, made unworthy and pitiable by the unworthiness of its idol. But even in the wildest of those moments she displayed an artist's control of herself and her resources.

XV.

ON THE ACTING OF LAWRENCE BARRETT.

LAWRENCE BARRETT'S impersonation of Ganelon — the hero of a four-act tragedy, in blank verse, by William Young — was the vital and sympathetic presentment of a type of chivalrous passion, tremulous intensity, and nervous force, and one of the most characteristic of his performances. It repeatedly afforded occasion for that tempest of vocal fervour upon which, by reason of a superb voice and an impassioned and melodious delivery, his art always rode so well; and it required culminative feeling and continuous and diversified action. At every point the actor was adequate to the part, and no observer of his performance could have missed the impression of intellectual authority, natural power, abundant theatrical equipment, and profound devotion to the stage.

One of the attributes that distinguish the actor from the experimenter, the elocutionist, and the novice is the faculty of

retrospective comprehension of character.
Every human being has a history — such
as it is. Behind every human being there
is a past; and the experience of that past
is recorded in each person's condition. In
order to understand what a man truly is it
is necessary to know what he has passed
through; what he has suffered; what he
has subdued; in what way he has conducted his life. Shakespeare's great characters owe their greatness to the fact, among
others, that they were comprehensively
conceived by him, each with its ample
background of experience. They are not
personifications of abstract ideas, cardinal
virtues, or cardinal vices; neither are they
theatrical puppets. The hero of a play,
supposing him to be substantial, must have
had his experience; and in the assumption
of him that is given by a true actor not
only his individuality will be expressed,
but the warp will be shown that his temperament has taken from the conditions of
his birth, his breeding, his circumstances,
his education, his vicissitudes, and his trials.
Lawrence Barrett was always conspicuously
fine in the felicity with which he grasped
his author's ideal, and the fidelity with
which, — taking that wide view of character,

— he conveyed it. When, for example, he paced upon the scene as Cassius, the whole background of the life of that austere Roman seemed to become visible. The intellectual majesty, the stern isolation, the cold aristocracy, the superb spirit, the unconquerable will, the exquisite refinement — all those qualities, fused into a type of proud ambition, iron purpose, and lonely grandeur, immediately suggested and defined a prodigious experience preliminary to such a result. No figures have stood upon the stage that are more sharply individualised, more distinct, more formidable, more readily remembered than those of Cassius, Harebell, Yorick, Lanciotto, and King James V. of Scotland, as presented by Lawrence Barrett. He saw them comprehensively ; he invested himself with their distinct personalities ; he made them actual men, while at the same time he sustained the element of charm in them by poetry of treatment in the expression of their characters.

To that group he added, in the same lofty spirit and with the same fine skill, the figure of Ganelon. This is a young French soldier, — a noble, ardent, impetuous, chivalrous gentleman, — whose youth has been clouded, whose spirit has been embittered, whose life has been violently wrenched from its natural posture and prospect, by the monstrous and afflicting disgrace of his father's discovered, manifest, irrefutable, murderous treason. That father was the Ganelon who betrayed Charlemagne's paladin Roland, — or Orlando, for he goes by both names — at Roncesvalles, in the Pyrenees, in 778, stipulating however, and successfully arranging, that his son should be spared the ensuing massacre. Young Ganelon, horror-stricken, and moving ever beneath a pall of unmerited infamy — the fatal inheritance of an ignominious name — has left his country and has wandered far, intent on a war of vengeance against the Saracens, then potent in Spain, to whom his father had delivered the paladins of Charlemagne. In the Corsican city of Aleria, which is besieged by those Saracens, he finds his opportunity — and also he finds his doom. Aleria has been summoned to surrender. The Christian Prince Colonna of Corsica has decreed a sortie, to defeat the assailing infidels and disperse them. A leader is required to head the desperate charge. Ganelon will be that leader — but he wishes, as a reward, in the event of victory, that he may be married to the Princess

Bianca, Colonna's daughter. That reward is promised, and thereupon he dashes furiously against the Saracens and scatters them in flight. But when he returns, to claim the royal and not unwilling bride, the Prince has listened to other counsel, and the reward is refused. Ganelon, crazed and desperate, utters a wild defiance and hurls himself to apparent and coveted death from a parapet of the royal town. He is not killed, however, by his fall, but he is captured by the Saracens, and thereupon tempted by their leader, Malec, and maddened by a passionate sense of the injustice of Colonna, he reveals to the recuperated invaders a secret passage into Aleria, and himself conducts them into the city, which is thus taken and devastated. Ganelon has now repeated — with a difference — the crime of his father. For a life thus accursed and blasted there can be but one refuge; and when, presently, the Princess Bianca, aware of his turpitude, repels Ganelon as a traitor, he is whirled into yet another frenzy, in which he kills the Moorish leader, Malec, rejoins the Christian Corsicans, and, fighting desperately, is wounded to death. In his last moments he has Bianca's forgiveness, and he dies with

the entrancing knowledge that if he had
lived he might have had her love — a consummation which, considering who he was
and how stigmatised, would have been a
misfortune for both of them.

The fact in human experience upon which
the structure of the play is reared is one that
has been often illustrated in the history of
the world and often enforced in works of
fiction. Injustice, acting upon pride and
sensibility in a brave, ardent, impetuous
nature, will sometimes disorganise, in that
nature, the foundations of moral principle;
will shatter reason and integrity; will create a bitter revulsion of feeling; and thus
will result in conduct which is only the
reckless, but which necessarily becomes the
cruel and afflicting, expression of resentment and fury. Coriolanus, ungratefully,
unjustly, meanly banished from the Rome
that he had saved and defended, joins with
the Volscians and leads them to victory over
his countrymen. Benedict Arnold, neglected and slighted by the military leaders
whom he had valorously served, deserts
the cause of Washington and madly heads
a crusade of sword and fire against his birthplace and his friends. With what magnificent power and to what splendid advantage

of immortal results the genius of Shakespeare has developed and applied the story of Coriolanus all thoughtful readers know. Benedict Arnold, whose story is full of meaning, has been put into drama, but not with success. In both those instances, however, there was a reflective consciousness, a coolness of purpose, that does not appear in the case of Ganelon — which is a case of malignant fate culminating in romantic frenzy.

The spectacle presented is that of pure tragedy. The sin of the father is visited upon the child. The endeavour of the youth to vindicate a dishonoured name is useless and hopeless from the beginning. Had he remained simply a soldier and devoted himself to the slaughter of Saracens he might perhaps have covered it with martial glory. When he became a lover and chose to be a suitor for a woman's hand — meaning to bring another life beneath the shadow of infamy unjustly, but not the less certainly, impending over his own — he encountered a fatal misfortune and made a selfish though unavoidable error. The visitation of love cannot be escaped. Conduct, however, can be regulated — unless there be a fate in the direction of events, as always is the case in

tragedy. Ganelon has great qualities, but
magnanimity and patience are not among
them. The mainspring of his temperament is
headlong impetuosity, and with him, as with
other human beings, escape from self is impossible. He is not to be blamed. He can
only be pitied. The tragedy is right in
making no attempt to readjust the inexorable laws of nature. The man is shown in
one picture after another of his intense re-
actions, his raptures, his explosive excite-
ments, his frenzies of reckless deed, — of
which the leap from the parapet of Aleria
is the sufficient exponent, — and the portraiture is dramatic. He is a fountain of
fiery life : it bursts through all restraint,
and its wasted splendours are scattered and
quenched upon the black water of death.
False by turns both to friend and enemy,
he is all the time true — for his acts are not
calculated treasons but insane paroxysms.
He keeps the observer's sympathy and pity
to the last ; and in the contemplation of
his pathetic and lamentable fate the mind
is conscious of that ennobling grief, — that
exalted commingling of terror at a mortal
catastrophe and pity for an inevitable ruin,
— which it is the distinctive province of
tragedy to cause.

The alienation of this story of a calamitous inheritance, a fatal love, a fatuous frenzy, and a pathetic death to the distant land of Corsica and to an historic period eleven hundred years ago might seem to have the effect of obscuring its outlines and deadening its significance. But as soon as the texture is examined it is found to be freshly interesting and replete with romantic elements; and, certainly, the writer of the tragedy has told it in a direct manner, — notwithstanding certain perilous interludes devoted to the Moors, — pointed his dramatic narrative with the emphatic effects of vigorous action, and written the needful soliloquies and colloquies in a fluent and polished strain of sonorous blank verse, that is an adequate vehicle for the conveyance of the piece.

Dramatic situations that authorise incessant and rapid movement and copious and vigorous eloquence were consonant with Lawrence Barrett's happiest mood as an actor, and were suited to his characteristic faculties. The draft upon the resources of the actor of Ganelon is incessant and severe. He must irradiate the spirit that makes the drama live. He is incarnate action. He is the electrical presence in every scene. Law-

rence Barrett pervaded the play, equally
with his personality and his polished art.
There was thought in the substance of all
that he achieved as an actor, and invariably there was delicate beauty in the form
and detail of his accomplishment. In his
expression of the horror and loathing with
which a noble spirit revolts from the iniquity of wedding a woman against her
will, he thrilled his hearers, and in the
scene of the attempted suicide his fine
impetuosity aroused a correspondent enthusiasm. The impersonation of Ganelon
created a new figure in the realm of stage
romance.

In the production of the tragedy a wealth
of pictorial scenery was used — to suggest
the warlike state of Corsica in a remote
historic period. Relief to the darkness of
a tragical theme was not afforded by at-
tempts at humour, but by action, incident,
processions, pictures, music, and the "pomp
and circumstance of glorious war." And
those were welcome. An observer who is
compelled to see much of the acted drama
grows weary of the heroes and heroines
who are impelled by sexual infatuation.
The changes have been rung upon that
theme to an everlasting extent — until it

almost seems as if there were nothing else
in the world but the sentimental pother
that precedes matrimony. Mature attention is apt to wander away from stage-
lovers. When it rested on such an actor
as Lawrence Barrett — admitting all his
fervour as Ganelon — it would have much
perferred to see him in Cassius or Coriolanus; past all the raptures and woes of
amatory passion, and supreme upon the
high and shining tablelands of the intellect
and the soul.

The moral lessons that are deducible
from stories of love that is false to its vows,
and of jealousy that culminates in deeds of
blood, are obvious and trite. It cannot be
supposed that the value, to a spectator, of
such a play as *Yorick* resides in its moral
lessons. Everybody knows that a breach
of the marriage contract is not justifiable
by the plea of a change of heart, even
though that change be natural and involuntary; and everybody knows that if
jealousy becomes madness and madness
commits murder the crime is one that
humanity in general will deplore rather
than condemn. A tragic play, to possess valuable import, must be more than
a rehearsal of platitudes or a reiteration

of the Ten Commandments. Nor does such a work become useful to others merely because it serves an actor as the vehicle for a felicitous manifestation of his professional skill. *Yorick* presents a spectacle of human trial and misery; and such a spectacle, faithfully copied from life and then transfigured in a work of art, will have power over the human heart and ennobling significance to the human mind, first by reason of sympathetic fidelity in its portraiture, and then by reason of its illumination of the conditions under which humanity is governed.

This tragedy, indeed, somewhat troubles the sense of justice by causing fatal consequences to flow from a venial and not a guilty fault; and perhaps its afflictive force is impaired by that error of construction. But as a picture of the pathetic, agonising, tragical entanglements which constantly arise in human experience it remains essentially and touchingly true. Here is a man of middle-age, a noble creature every way, whose being is absorbed with the passion of love for his young wife: here is a young woman, naturally good, who has married an elderly man, out of kindness and affection, only to find, too late, that marriage must rest on a far more imperious feeling: here is the handsome young lover who, in complete innocence and without volition, awakens the woman's heart and readily wins it from a husband who is merely respected: and here is wicked enmity personified in a soured and embittered man, smarting under that wound to vanity which low and common natures can never bear and will never forgive. It is an old, old story; but even without ingenuity of plot and felicity of dramatic treatment and of language, it would possess an impressive meaning. The thing to contemplate is the situation — the relation to each other into which innocent persons are driven, by no act of their own — the terrible hardships that fate imposes on them and the awful catastrophe that inevitably ensues. The youthful lovers cannot help either their passion or their anguish. The poor old actor, fallen into the sear and yellow, cannot help his frantic jealousy, his despair, his madness, his rash acts of fatal retribution. No attempt is made to soften those facts of life. Facts they are, and experience vouchsafes no comment on those grim pictures of disaster. All we can know is that the story of human life is full of such events, and that the highest wisdom, and only possible refuge, is endurance. *Yorick* succeeded because it paints the life of the passions truthfully, and speaks simply this word to illumine its picture.

Lawrence Barrett, in *Yorick*, was adequate at every point, and he gave a noble and touching performance. His ideal of the comedian, who deeply feels the serious aspect of life and would like to play tragedy, was especially right and fine in this respect, among others, that it was precisely the sort of man whom a commonplace young woman would like but could neither love nor understand. The gentle humility of a fine nature was expressed by him with sweet and natural self-depreciation, so that *Yorick* was made wistful, and he would have been almost forlorn but for his guileless trust and his blithe, eager, childlike spirit. An ordinary girl would be flattered by the love of such a man, and would be quite content with him, as long as she did not love somebody else. The pitiable character of this disparity was especially enforced, though indirectly — which was all the better art — by the free play, the abandonment, that was given to an honest, confiding, simple, happy heart. *Yorick*, indeed, was made to talk too much when his hour of trial and misery came; but that was the fault of the writer and not the actor. Sorrow speaks little. Macduff, in one of the great master's scenes, simply pulls his hat upon his brows. Lawrence Barrett proved his signal power by the splendid self-control and the refined art with which he subordinated copious declamation to intense feeling; and thus he taught the wisdom of Wordsworth's fine precept:

> "Keep, ever keep, as if by touch
>   Of self-restraining art,
> The modest charm of not too much—
>   Part seen, imagined part."

XVI.

WOLFERT'S ROOST AND RAYMOND.

"THE artist," says Longfellow, "shows his character in the choice of his subject." In choosing from Washington Irving the subject of *Wolfert's Roost*, George Fawcett Rowe evinced a characteristic sympathy with what is quaint, humorous, gentle, and romantic in literature and life. The field into which he thus penetrated has not, for this purpose, been much explored. *Rip Van Winkle* — remotely of Greek and later of German origin — was found in it; and one at least of the tales of the *Alhambra* has been turned into a play. There are other instances; but that rich realm of fiction has been neglected. Irving was the father of our literature. His hand laid the foundation of the graceful structure of letters that is slowly rising in the nation. The sneer of Rogers, that he was only "Addison and water," and the contemptuous estimate of Hazlitt, who called him "a mere filigree man," were long ago discomfited; and it is a pleasant spectacle that the stage presents when it enriches itself, and fosters and benefits the public taste, at the same time that it pays a tribute to the memory of the first of American authors. Irving, indeed, is not a dramatic writer. The charm of his stories resides in feeling, description, character, and style. They do not attempt action, and they contain but little dialogue. Yet they are vital with the play of ingenious fancy, and they abound in suggestions of situation. The dramatist would do no good in merely reproducing them. He must expand their hints, embody their descriptions, amplify their outlines of character, rearrange their incidents, and vitalise with action the structure of their plots. There is no better dramatic subject than the subject of *Rip Van Winkle;* and a much better play could be made out of it than the careless rearrangement of the old piece which only the genius of Jefferson has kept alive. Rowe selected the narrower and humbler theme of *Ichabod Crane;* but he wrought with fine ability and conscientious skill and he made one of the most pleasing domestic plays in the language. Its story is round, coherent, sympathetic, and its five acts tell its story in action, without excess

of words. Its characters are clearly dis-
criminated, and each is harmonious with
probability, with itself, and with the historical period (about 1812), in which the
scene is cast. Its movement is continuous,
through a series of dramatic effects, to a
striking climax and a happy culmination.
Its plot — expanded out of hints from *Wolfert's Roost, The Legend of Sleepy Hollow,*
and other writings of Irving — if not new,
is commended to favour by novelty of treatment. Its incidents are numerous and,
generally, are bright. Its method in displaying the central character of Ichabod
Crane, — who is made a sort of lovable
Paul Pry, or a sprightly and energetic
Dominie Sampson, — shows a delightful
nimbleness of fancy, and a hearty relish of
quaint and droll humour. Its sentiment is
tender; its spirit is pure; and over it all
there is an atmosphere of romance, deftly
and softly commingled with rustic colour.
Its scene is mostly out-of-doors, and in its
use of night and day, foliage, moonlight,
storm, flowers, sound, and silence, it shows
a deep and fine feeling for the charms and
the mysteries of nature. Its dialogue —
almost entirely original with the dramatist,
who has taken but a few sentences from

Irving — is unaffected, suitable to the subject and the several speakers, and at times pungent with a felicitous wit. "You never was a fader?" says old Balthus to Brom Brones. "No, and I never shall be," answers the baffled suitor of Katrina, "if I go on like this." "Beauty is but skin deep," says Ichabod Crane. "That's deep enough, isn't it?" is the responsive inquiry of Katrina. Pure drama it is — and not comedy. There is no attempt to paint manners, nor to idealise types of society, nor to enliven artificial talk with the sheen of equivoke. Customs, indeed, are suggested — as when, in act third, the characters assemble in "the living-room" of the farm-house to frolic on All-Hallow E'en. The fragrance of old-time civilisation, in what was still Dutch New York, is made to saturate the texture of the piece. But, manifestly, the work was made for its own sake — for its story, character, and vehicular utility in acting — and not for the illumination of its epoch. And it was made well. There are a few defects of forced incident and untrue character. The fibre of the piece is slender; and, by reason more of the subject of the drama than the author's treatment of it, the work is wanting in that vitality which comes of everlasting applicability to common experience, that universality of interest which alone can give permanence to the creations of the human mind. Yet it is a charming play. Its first act confronts Dolph Haverstraw and Brom Van Brunt as lovers of Katrina Van Tassel. Dolph is heir to the impoverished estate of *Wolfert's Roost;* Brom is a flourishing young butcher; Katrina, the blooming daughter of Baltus Van Tassel, is the belle of Sleepy Hollow. Those persons, together with Dolph's mother and sister, Phœbe, a mulatto servant, Ichabod Crane, the comic factotum of his neighbourhood, and "the grimly ghost" of old Wolfert Haverstraw, are all brought on in this act, and the story is opened by the dispatch of Dolph to sea, and the apparition of the Dutch spectre, seen by Ichabod, and heard to command a search for his buried treasure. The rising of the Ghost from an old well ends this act, and makes a weirdly fantastic picture. Act second shows Katrina grieving for the absent Dolph, whom she has petulantly rejected; Ichabod — smitten by the heiress — comically striving to learn the cause of her sadness; Emma

Haverstraw enamoured of Ichabod ; and,
finally, Brom Bones exultant in the news
that his rival has been lost at sea. Acts
third and fourth, beginning with the in-
timation that this bad news is not true,
are devoted to rejoicings at Van Tassel's
farm, and involve Dolph's return, in
disguise, Emma's betrothal to Ichabod, a
comical rendering of the episode of *The
Headless Hessian* — wherein Ichabod is
hit with a hurtling pumpkin, and knocked
into Wolfert's well — and the burning
of Wolfert's Roost and attempted murder of Dolph by the jealous and infuri-
ated Brom Van Brunt. The last act
brings to light and to punishment the iniquity of Van Brunt, unites Dolph and
Katrina, and produces Ichabod — who
has come up from the bottom of the
well with old Wolfert's buried treasure.
There is a shuddering passage in the last
act, wherein the superstitious dread of
Brom Bones, who thinks himself haunted
by a murdered man, is used with wild
power to wind up the play. Ichabod
Crane pervades the piece, and lights it up
with his humour and good-nature. He is
ungainly, agile, pertinacious, fantastic, absurd and ludicrous ; yet tender, delicate,

and lovable — a compound of awkward gallantry, Quixotic philanthropy, scarecrow drollery, shrewd sense, and homespun refinement. That part requires a keen sense of comic perplexity, a touch of wistful tenderness here and there — his condition is so forlorn — and, in one scene, an emotion closely akin to pathos. It was acted by John T. Raymond, and that rare comedian found it a thoroughly congenial part: he infused into it a sweet spirit, and he treated it with a delicacy of touch that surprised many who had known him only as the vociferous Sellers. To some extent the part is extraneous to the main action of the drama. It hovers around the current of what is done and suffered, but is not interpenetrated with those experiences. Moreover, in the enforced transfer of his love, wrought by the coquettish Katrina, Ichabod is cajoled, and that limits the scope of the character, in serious acting. Raymond, all the same, embodied a winning personality, and made it as gracious with inherent gentleness as it was droll with eccentric humour.

XVII.

MANSFIELD IN SEVERAL CHARACTERS.

ROBERT LOUIS STEVENSON'S grotesque and grisly story of the *Strange Case of Dr. Jekyll and Mr. Hyde* was published in 1885. As a literary composition it is fragmentary, almost curtly written, and roughly jointed. The form intended was the form of the documentary memorandum. There are readers who will think that a conception so fine and so absorbing ought to have been considerably expanded and symmetrically shaped, and that its text — which reads like a first draft — ought to have been carefully written. Nevertheless it is a work of originality and power, and one for which — as for all works of originality and power, in days of excessive criticism — everybody should be grateful. That such a story should have suggested a play is not surprising. Yet it is purely narrative in structure, and its dramatic elements are, as a chemist would say, in solution. Facts and incidents are merely stated. The culmination of the plot is reached in the middle of the narrative and is then supplemented with an explanation. Perhaps, also, the testimony and the description would have been truer to human nature, and thus more directly in the vein of the dramatist, had the author made a more thoroughly logical analysis of his conception. Perhaps the Dr. Jekyll whom he has described is a sort of man who would be but little likely to take the mystic and transcendental track and turn into Mr. Hyde, and perhaps no man, having once travelled that dark road, could afterward exist without giving more numerous and more harrowing denotements of it — even in the brief interval that precedes his ruin and extinction — than are given by the Dr. Jekyll of the book. However that may be, the story has been turned into a tragic drama, which is alert with incident, rapid and cumulative with action, various in character, fluent in style, and significant in picture and in meaning. The play was planned and sketched by Richard Mansfield and made by Thomas R. Sullivan. It had its first representation on May 9, 1887, at the Museum in Boston.

The thought upon which Stevenson built

his story, and which likewise is made to sustain the fabric of the play, is stated in the words of the novelist, here extracted from Dr. Jekyll's confession:

"I saw that, of the two natures that contended in the field of my consciousness, even if I could rightly be said to be either, it was only because I was radically both. . . . I learned to dwell with pleasure, as a beloved day-dream, on the thought of the separation of these elements. If each could be housed in separate identities, life would be relieved of all that was unbearable. . . . I began to perceive . . . the trembling immateriality, the mist-like transience, of this seemingly so solid body in which we walk attired. Certain agents I found to have the power to shake and to pluck back that fleshy vestment, even as a wind might toss the curtains of a pavilion. . . . I not only recognised my natural body for the mere aura and effulgence of certain of the powers that made up my spirit, but managed to compound a drug by which these powers should be dethroned from their supremacy, and a second form and countenance substituted, none the less natural to me because they were the expression and bore the stamp of lower elements in my soul."

In the allegorical sense there is a basis of significant truth in that fantastic reasoning. Human nature is composite. Human goodness would sink supine in sloth if there were not evil in the warp of things to compel it to action — evil being the agent in creation that never rests and cannot rest. Many persons, no doubt, go through life without ever once lapsing into vicious conduct. But most persons who from the summit of middle life look back upon the past are aware that they have sometimes had the consciousness of evil moods and impulses — a tendency in themselves so wrong that, had it ripened into wicked acts, instead of ending in the conquest of good over bad, it would have alienated them from their better nature, and thus might almost be said to have changed their identity. When a good man consciously does wrong he has, for the time, ceased to be his actual self. The man who keeps on consciously doing wrong must eventually blunt his moral sense and weaken his power of resistance to evil, till at last he becomes incapable of reverting to his former state of virtue. The old theologians called that catastrophe the ultimate triumph of " original sin." The scientists of to-day declare it to be the temporary predominance of that remnant of the brute in the human which evolution has not yet entirely eradicated.

In order to build a play upon this minute allegory of imagined, emblematic experience it was necessary, first, to reject the intention to dramatise the book in such a manner as to reproduce it, and, secondly, to devise a scheme of innovation upon the original. There is a narrow order of the critical mind which, in a case of this sort, seems to feel a savage delight at finding discrepancies betwixt the play and the novel upon which the play is founded. Of course there are discrepancies. They exist in every similar case ; they are inevitable ; and, furthermore, they are essential. Just as a lecturer is not an actor, although each may treat a dramatic theme, so a novel is not a play, although both may relate to the same subject. The novel describes. The play exhibits. The novel is character in picture, clothed with description. The play is character in action, clothed with scenery. Once in a while somebody writes a novel so dramatic that it can, with just a few touches, be turned into a play ; but that is rare. More often the novel must be greatly altered before its dramatic aspects can be released. Frequently portions of its material must be rejected to make way for material absolutely new. That was the necessity of the case in dealing with *Dr. Jekyll and Mr. Hyde*. The dramatist took the essential idea of the book, its ground plan and its dramatic situations and incidents; but he modified its characters and displayed them under changed conditions, and he environed *the Strange Case* as well with an atmosphere of domestic life and love as with the otherwise unrelieved and monotonous investiture of weirdness and horror.

The movement begins in the home of Sir Danvers Carew, who is present in company with his daughter and their guests. Among the latter are Mr. Utterson and Dr. Lanyon. The time is evening and the scene is one of domestic comfort and repose. The theme of the play is opened by a talk between Dr. Lanyon and Mr. Utterson, in which Hyde and his savage cruelty are described. Dr. Jekyll comes upon this scene — a pale, sad man, forlorn and wistful, over whom it is instantly observed that trouble has cast an indescribable blight. But Dr. Jekyll and Agnes Carew, the

daughter of Sir Danvers Carew, are be-
trothed lovers, and it is intimated that they
are soon to wed. The girl cheers her
lover, and will not hear his self-reproachful
words. Presently the scene is cleared of
all but Sir Danvers Carew and Agnes, who
linger awhile, in affectionate talk of the
past. Just as they have said good-night,
and are parting, the grisly and sinister
figure of Hyde, emerging from the moonlight, glides into the room, through a great
window at the back of it — a figure like
Jekyll, yet most unlike him; shrunken,
malevolent, repulsive, stealthy, insolent in
demeanour, horrible in facial expression,
irritating in voice, a loathsome image of
depravity and menace. This wretched
reptile coarsely commands the father to
call back his daughter, and being repelled
by the intrepid baronet, suddenly springs
upon him and chokes and mauls him to
death. The spectacle is very hideous, but
happily it is soon over. Mansfield is an
artist, and he did not linger upon any point
once made.

The second act consists of three scenes.
Hyde is shown in his secret lodging, where,
with blood-curdling glee, he fills a cup of
wine and pledges the ghost of Sir Dan-

vers Carew. Mansfield wisely and widely
deviated from the novel, by surround-
ing this miscreant with profuse, disorderly
luxury — not that of taste, but that of exuberant sensuality — such as Ben Jonson
indicates for Volpone and Sir Epicure
Mammon. This scene shows the police in
pursuit of Hyde, and ends with his escape
through a secret door, artfully devised
within a mirror. He is next encountered
entering the mysterious postern of Dr.
Jekyll's cabinet, and there he is accosted
by Utterson. The subsequent scene is
within the cabinet, and Dr. Jekyll once
more becomes the central figure. Act
third is occupied with the startling scene in
Dr. Lanyon's house wherein Hyde mixes
and swallows his drug and is visibly trans-
formed into Jekyll. In act fourth Dr. Jekyll,
immured in his cabinet, and shuddering
on the verge of involuntary transformation into the brute that lurks within him,
beseeches Dr. Lanyon to bring Agnes beneath the window, so that he can look
upon her face for the last time. Jekyll is
now doomed, and his better nature must take
leave of all things that are good and lovely
in the world. The tragedy and the pathos
of it are that the parting is eternal. The

girl is brought, but at the moment when he looks upon her the transformation is accomplished, and the imbruted Hyde — aware of his danger — swallows a quick poison and sprawls horribly into death.

In any field of art the portraiture of the monstrous is comparatively easy. A good actor can fill the measure of Caliban more readily than he can fill the measure of Lear. But the portraiture of the monstrous, if comparatively easy, is superlatively fruitless. Doubtless it enables the actor to make a startling display of his skill. The monstrous is almost always powerful. It is the crocodile or the cobra, and it frightens, or sickens, or horrifies. But a spectator derives no lasting benefit from a display of power and skill in that direction. Horror is barren, except of disgust. E. L. Davenport, in the full maturity of his extraordinary powers, set out to achieve a national popularity by playing Sir Giles Overreach. He played it marvellously well, and his great ability in it was recognised and admired; but, the better his performance was the more it was avoided. The character is a monster, and being merely monstrous it is hateful. Such creations, devoid of a human side — being neither brilliant, fascinating, conscience-stricken and rueful, like Richard III., nor awful and pathetic, like the fiend-driven Macbeth — cannot be redeemed and commended to sympathy by any felicity, however great, of artistic treatment. Henry Irving's great performance of Dubosc — who, however, is more a human savage than a monster — derives its greatness partly from the actor's humour, but far more from its association with that superb image of beautiful purity and lofty heroism, the companion character of Lesurques, which is concurrently embodied by that man of genius. The two works are taken together, and they are felt and accepted as a wonderful and thrilling example of the variety of attributes which may exist within the scope of one and the same human mind. It is not simply a hideous aspect of reptile vitality that awakens sympathy and wins admiration ; it is the potency of that manifold, impressive, and touching significance which is expressed and conveyed in the correlation of beautiful and terrible attributes in one and the same being, and that being a human creature.

Mansfield depicted, with horrible animal vigour and with intense and reckless force of infernal malignity, the exultant wickedness of the bestial and frenzied Hyde — displaying a carnal monster of unqualified evil. It was an assumption remarkable for intensity and prodigious power. That actor possesses great volume of voice and great impetuosity of nervous force, and his acting of Hyde, viewed simply as execution, furnished conclusive evidence of his exceptional resources and proficiency in the dramatic art. But Mansfield rose to a nobler height than that — for he was able, in the concurrent and associate impersonation of Dr. Jekyll, to interblend the angel with the demon, and thus to command a lasting victory, such as his baleful image of the hellish Hyde could never, separately, achieve. That is the basis of his remarkable success. He was distinctly individual in each of the characters. His dramatic art and his temperamental quality were as cogent in the one as in the other. But by concurrently embodying the two, — by at once contrasting his two studies and blending them into one, — he displayed, under dramatic circumstances of unique and unflagging interest, a single image of human nature — the image of a man who is convulsed, lacerated, and ultimately destroyed by a terrific and fatal struggle, upon the theatre of his own soul and body, between inherent forces of good and evil. The two works taken together enthralled the imagination and deeply touched the heart. The presentment was an awful and pathetic picture of a remorseful human soul overwhelmed by the sin to which it has yielded, while struggling to avert the terrible consequences of its self-murder. The actor's art diffused the unfailing charm of spontaneous dramatic action, and in its magnetic quality and its strong enforcement of the essential moral truth that the deadliest peril of the immortal spirit lies in successive surrender to conscious iniquity it was a distinct revelation of genius.

Three points might especially be indicated at which Mansfield conspicuously manifested imagination, creative dramatic power, and sympathetic emotion. The sardonic malignity of Hyde, when he pledges the ghost of Sir Danvers Carew, the inspired exultation with which Hyde, controlled by Jekyll, exhorts Dr. Lanyon before drinking the magical mixture, and the afflicting pathos of Jekyll when, as he takes his eternal farewell of beauty and goodness and life, he gathers into his hands a few flowers and tenderly gives them a parting caress, were in the most exalted mood of acting. The actor's transitions, also, were wonderfully fine. In act third Hyde changes to Jekyll. In act fourth Jekyll changes to Hyde. The transformation was wrought in physical bearing, in stature and demeanour, in facial expression, and above all, in what can only be indicated as the radiation of an interior spirit. As denotements at once of the man's soul and the artist's faculty that effect was eloquent and impressive in no common degree.

But the essential and abiding superiority of Mansfield's impersonation was in his fine analysis of the nature of Dr. Jekyll and his adjustment of that nature to its terrible and lamentable conditions. Here were involved the retrospective quality, — the quality in acting which discloses a whole life-time in a single glimpse, — the sympathy, the redeeming humanity, the poetry, in one word the justification of the whole work. Dr. Jekyll in the book never inspires sympathy, but he constantly wins it in the play. Stevenson marks him out as "a large, well-made, smooth-faced man of fifty, with something of a sly cast, perhaps, but every mark of capacity and kindness";

and Stevenson makes him say: "It was rather the exacting nature of my own aspirations than any particular degradation in my faults that made me what I was and severed in me those provinces of good and ill which divide and compound man's dual nature." That recalls Brinsley Sheridan's standard of virtue, — which he said was so high that he could not possibly live up to it. Mansfield both rectified and exalted the ethics of the subject by his finer ideal of Jekyll — who, a poetic enthusiast for occult science, has conjured up a spectre that he cannot lay and subjected himself to an impending doom that he cannot, by any self-sacrifice or expiation, avert. There are certain works — and works of merit, too — that stop short at personal display of the actor. They are pyrotechnics, brilliant while burning, but gone for ever as soon as they cease to burn. The supreme merit of Mansfield's impersonation of Jekyll and Hyde was that it transcended personal display; that it came home to every human heart and had a meaning for every human soul.

There were technical defects. The tones of Jekyll's voice were often metallic. The love scenes lacked passion. It was not till the death scene that the face of Jekyll seemed wholly true to his nature. The aspect of Hyde was over-gruesome, suggesting that of a gnome in a fairy spectacle. It ought to be sinister and deadly — for dramatic purposes — and possessed of the hideous fascination of the adder.

All persons are glad to see Mansfield who honour the element of mind, who respect high purpose and noble ambition, and who exult in the achievements of genius. The lovers of novelty, likewise, are captured by his approach, and they find pleasure in his presence. All things conspired to make the occasion of his production of *The Scarlet Letter* (Sept. 13, 1892, at Daly's Theatre) imposing with mental effort and brilliant with social interest. He made, indeed, a fruitless expenditure of his fine powers upon a frail, sombre, monotonous, and inconclusive play and upon a weak part ; but he did that with the same sincerity and skill, the same artistic authority and personal force that have invariably characterised his public proceedings, and his achievement, therefore, commanded respect. Arthur Dimmesdale is not a good acting part, and the actor who derives so much effect from it as Mansfield did must be accredited with extraordinary individuality and charm.

The message of *The Scarlet Letter* is an abortive and useless message of misery. The story depicts the misery of a woman whom love has brought to public shame; the misery of a clergyman who — until he becomes moribund — is not brave enough to cease to be a hypocrite, and who suffers and slowly dies beneath the pressure of remorse; and, finally, the misery of a repudiated husband — deformed in person, old, crafty, malignant — who sees his idolised wife an adulteress, and who pursues the most hideous and awful scheme of revenge upon her lover that colossal hatred can prompt or the utmost refinement of intellect accomplish. And nothing comes of it. If a vital drama could be derived from that classical epitome of romantic sin and sorrow the audience would no doubt be edified by that exploit; for, as an historic picture, the romance is instructive, while as a weird and subtle analysis of human nature it is impressive to the imagination; and the style of it is beautiful. In the narrative form it has reached and moved many readers, and it always will command a certain public. The scope of drama, how-

ever, is wider than that of narrative, and
the portraiture and emotion of that work
might be carried much further than they
have ever been carried yet if it could be
turned into a powerful play. The multitude would then learn more than it has
known, or is likely to know, of the genius
of Hawthorne. But the dramatic element
— that is to say, the element of doing — is
not conspicuous in *The Scarlet Letter*, and
that element cannot rightfully be wrought
into its texture. The principal persons
who are implicated in the fiction are inert
persons. They watch each other and they
suffer, but they do not move. Mr. Joseph
Hatton has done everything that could be
done with the materials at his command.
His play is an excellent synopsis of the
story. The structural incidents of the
original are included. The characters are
reproduced. The situation that Hawthorne
invented was duly displayed. The catastrophe that occurs in the book was represented
on the stage. Every spectator who had
read the romance could follow the line of
the drama. The exposure of Hester upon
the pillory, Chillingworth's discovery of
Dimmesdale's secret, the discomfiture of
the plan of escape, and at last the confes-

sion and death of the minister, were all
wrought into the fabric of the piece ; and,
without discredit to its gloomy austerity,
a certain sprightliness was imparted to it
by an adroit elucidation of the captain of
the Bristol ship and also of those iron-vis-
aged dames whom Hawthorne assembled
around Hester's scaffold. The thing that
was not reproduced, and could not be reproduced, is Hawthorne's intellectual and
spiritual treatment of his subject, in which
the chief value of the book consists.
Neither by means of Hawthorne's spirit,
however, nor by any other means, could
the piece have been made anything else
than a picture. It is motionless. That was
inevitable. And it was inevitable, furthermore, that the play should be as didactic as
it is stationary.

Every bad deed is succeeded, sooner or
later, by its commensurate punishment.
Penalty follows crime. If the offence be
committed against the laws of society,
those laws will punish the offender — when
they reach him. If the sin be committed
against the soul, it is registered in memory,
and it becomes a perpetual torture. Truths
of this order make the basis of *The Scarlet
Letter* and are inculcated by it. A por-

trayal of spiritual struggles and sufferings under weird and darkly picturesque historic conditions was the author's object when he told that story and declared those truths. That portrayal, in the narrative, is vitalised with grim and ghastly speculation, and with a thousand light and subtle touches of detail, enhanced by a fantastic play of fancy — as when rank weeds growing out of a grave are denoted as symbols of unacknowledged sins of the creature mouldering beneath them. The reader, perceiving this tone and drift, supplies the necessary action — supposing him to be interested in the subject at all. That portrayal, in drama, on the contrary, becomes mere pictorial reflection. Endurance is silent. Suffering does not act. It may, indeed, talk — as it does in the immortal blank verse of *Hamlet;* but even so, it will be dull and heavy unless its accents fall from lips that genius has inspired to utter the universal language of the heart. To predominate by deed, to sway by means of action, to reveal character projecting itself into conduct under the stress of impulse and circumstance — that is forbidden to sufferers. Arthur Dimmesdale passed seven wretched years in pretending to be holy

before the world, while in secret he was all
the time writhing under the agony of remorse and wasting away with the canker
of grief. To think of a miserable man, thus
weak and thus burdened, dying silently and
by inches beneath the cold, patient, stealthy,
inevitable eye of a secret, malignant, and
most fatal enemy, is to form an ideal of
dreadful suffering and of deadly peril, and
also it is to shudder at a grisly image of
baleful depravity. But to look upon the
actual spectacle is simply to see two men in
two chairs. The concrete image dissipates
emotion by substituting a bald fact for a
terrible imagining.

A play, in order that it may be effective,
must concern itself with physics and not
with metaphysics. In this instance its
legitimate concern is with the circumstances and doings of two lovers and their
enemy, and not with the several phases of
mental perturbation through which each
one of those persons painfully works a
tortuous and tiresome passage. Those two
lovers are a handsome and highly intellectual young clergyman and the youthful
and beautiful wife of an unpleasant old
scholar who had been thought to be dead.
Those lovers, under irresistible temptation,

have fallen into sin, and for that error they have dreadfully suffered. The woman has been disgraced, and the man has languished beneath the puissant malice of the revengeful husband, who has lived with him as a friend and has insidiously striven to torture him to madness. At length the lovers resolve to fly away from their doom of torment and dwell at peace together, but their purpose is discovered and baffled. Then the minister publicly confesses his guilt, and — worn out with anguish — expires upon the pillory. The wife and husband, aliened forever, remain to suffer longer. That is the substance of the piece — and trite and frail enough that substance is, as material for a play. The spectator, however, like the dramatist, must make the most of it — taking comfort in the thought that Hawthorne was a great writer, and that *The Scarlet Letter* is esteemed his greatest work. The sympathy of such a spectator naturally goes with the woman. She had been wrongfully wedded. She had been long parted from her obnoxious husband. She had lost her heart, and she had naturally, though sinfully, followed where it went. She was branded with ignominy and devoted to a life of laborious expiation.

Furthermore, her environment was that of colonial New-England. She lived in Boston, in the age when the blue lights were in full blast. Hawthorne himself seems to have been sorry for her, but Hawthorne's morality was entirely conventional.

The Iagos and the Macbeths of dramatic literature are perfectly feasible by dramatic art. An actor need not have done a murder in order to be qualified to impersonate a murderer. Yet, in his imagination, he must be capable of the feeling that accompanies the crime, while in his temperament he must be consonant with that feeling. The Shepherd of Salisbury Plain would not do for Iago. The Cheeryble Brothers would not do for Hamlet and Richard. In other words, no man is capable of depicting or suggesting in art a spiritual experience of which he is incapable in life. Mansfield's mind and temperament have little or no affinity with those of Arthur Dimmesdale. The actor is alert, robust, impetuous, vital. His interest in life is obviously very strong. He is naturally prone to enterprise, and is fond of it. His executive faculties are prodigious. He is both combative and wayward, and his most characteristic mental mood is that of satirical humour. His nature, indeed, includes elements of pensive sweetness, poetic repose, and tender pathos; but careful observance of his acting discerns that those elements are, for the present, subsidiary, and that sterner and brisker qualities predominate over them. Arthur Dimmesdale is a weak, irresolute, morbid man, a moral coward, a narrow religionist, concentrated on himself, and self-consumed with remorseful brooding over a spiritual sin. Such an actor as Mansfield could actually and fully and persuasively impersonate such an ideal only by the complete effacement of his identity, the utter obliteration of every characteristic attribute of his nature. This is something that never happens to anybody, and it cannot be expected to occur with him. His success consisted in the display of passionate earnestness, the expression of deep tenderness, and therewithal an artful simulation of suppressed excitement, at times breaking all bounds and bursting forth in frenzy. Perception of Dimmesdale — his love, his grief, his vague apprehension, his spiritual conflict, his occasional paroxysms of delirious revolt — the actor obviously possessed; and that he made manifest in a pallid, pictur-

esque, emaciated, loquacious image of
lachrymose grief. But the part was neither
kindred with his quality nor commensurate
with his powers. He played it well. He
could not raise it above its natural level.
His abrupt, spasmodic action when repuls-
ing the officious physician, his midnight
apostrophe upon the scaffold, and his final
effort, at the confession speech, were superb.
At those points his remarkable voice rang
out like a clarion, and his eloquence had
the thrill of intense emotion.

A man who loves — if he is to interest
others — should have the courage of his
love. If there is shame to be met he should
be willing to meet it. He should not leave
the woman to bear it. Above all, he should
not leave the woman to bear it alone.
There is something contemptible in the
character of Dimmesdale, and the more
clearly he is delineated the more contemptible he seems. For the art of acting
the most fruitful character in *The Scarlet
Letter* manifestly is Chillingworth. In this
man's nature resentment against the cruelty
of fate has engendered the malignity of a
fiend. His aspect is calm, but the fires of
hell are burning in his bosom. He is pru-
dent, vigilant, self-contained, but he is rest-

less underneath his mask, and his inveterate purpose shows itself in a continuous vivisection of his victim. He is forever weaving his web ; forever closing the avenues of escape ; forever preparing to strike the final blow — whereof the consequences are to reach beyond the grave. He is specious, subtle, and deadly. He aims to avenge himself, not by killing the body, but — if that is possible — by killing the soul. The settled belief that eternal damnation awaits the soul of a sinner, sent to his account with the burden upon him of unconfessed and unexpiated sin, is at the basis of his mind and conduct, and it is essential to the infernal purpose and hellish fabric of his design. The moment when that fatal man uncovers the breast of the sleeping sufferer, and beholds the scarlet letter that has been hidden there (in the play this was artfully made to occur on the scaffold at night), is a moment of tragedy as terrible as it is true ; and it is a moment that only a tragedian could illumine and sustain. Certainly the character of Chillingworth is unsympathetic. No audience would ever be humanly fascinated with the image of a man who is striving to augment and prolong the torments of a sinner in this world and to procure the damnation of his soul in the world to come; yet it is not difficult to perceive that, if there were an adequate scheme of action for him to bustle in, an actor of genius and of consummate art might invest that personality with attributes that would make it both piteous and awful.

The personality and the temperament of Hester Prynne might be deduced from her conduct — even if they had not been clearly denoted by the author. She is tall, sumptuous, elegant. She has abundant dark and glossy hair, strongly marked brows, and black eyes. Her features are regular, her complexion is pure and rich, her voice is deep and gentle, her deportment is stately, and she moves with dignity. Her feelings are intense and she is remarkably self-contained. Only on a few occasions — as when the legal authorities propose to assume the custody of her child, and when she warns Dimmesdale of the presence of the enemy at his hearthstone — does she yield to her emotions and outwardly display the tremendous passion of her soul. She is all woman and one of the highest types of her sex. The part, however, is made to depend on presence, not action, and therefore is impracticable.

XVIII.

ADA REHAN'S ACTING.

IN the records that remain of the famous women of the stage there is but little that interprets, and there is nothing that perpetuates, their charm. The biographies, for example, that commemorate Mrs. Porter, Mrs. Pritchard, Mrs. Bracegirdle, Mrs. Oldfield, Mrs. Dancer, Mrs. Cibber, Mrs. Woffington, Mrs. Yates, and Mrs. Siddons, while they are profuse and sometimes enthusiastic in specification of the exploits and the particular triumphs of those illustrious actors, may be said to designate the secret of their power rather than to display it. When all has been told that words can tell of those delicious combinations of genius and beauty, there is still something which remains untold. The enchanting allurement of eyes and voice, the fascination of individuality, the charm of temperament, the puissant sympathetic force, the spell of inspiration, — those attributes cannot be crystallised into the written word.

The biographer can only declare that they existed ; their magical loveliness and their triumphant sway must be imagined by the reader. Whenever those attributes are present in a person who can be seen and heard, they are hailed with acclamation ; but they perish even with the plaudits they excite. The past exulted in many dramatic idols ; the present has inherited only their names. So it has ever been and so it will be forever. Admirable dramatic leaders of the present will doubtless be known to the future, but they will be known as shadows. Their fame may fly onward : the reason for it will remain behind. What words can transmit to posterity the smile of Ellen Terry or the voice of Ada Rehan ?

The pictorial art has done much for actors, — more than could be done for them by the art of writing. The best understood and most admired actor of the past is David Garrick ; and that is mainly because many portraits were made of him, which still survive, — most of them good, and many of them superbly illuminative of what must indeed have been an enchanting face. To the pictorial art, accordingly, judgment, taste, and friendship, will resort when they

are wishful to commemorate an actor.
Portraits of Ada Rehan would tell more
about her than can be told in words, for
they would take a wide range, and therein
they would denote the versatility which is
one of her prominent characteristics. They
would show her in heroines of Shakespeare ; in the women of old English comedy ; in characters of modern comedy
— a theatrical fabric much tinged with
farce — and in characters that are almost
tragical. She has assumed at least a hundred and fifty characters, since she went
upon the stage. She has been eminently
successful, and the field of thought in
which, obviously, she must have deeply
studied — is extensive, diversified, and important ; so that her success is an eloquent
denotement of her elemental power and her
various ability. In the experience of Ada
Rehan, however, as in that of other actors, it
has been found that the dramatic faculty becomes, in time, defined and restricted as to
its natural and therefore its best expression
by peculiarities and limitations of temperament, which assign it to special types of
human nature and to various modifications
of them. Miss Rehan did not begin at the
top, but humbly, in a minor character and

at a provincial theatre; and from that
lowly station she has risen to the rank of
leading woman in the leading theatre of
America, — a high position and one that
rests upon a foundation of more solid
achievement than many of the stars of this
period have found essential to their fame.
In that progress she has developed an original and brilliant personality, and by her
natural aptitude for the mood of buoyant
raillery which plays over a depth of tender
feeling she has proved herself born for the
province of the comedian.

The American stage, viewing it as a
national institution, has only of late years
become an independent power. It was
built by British actors. The moment you
begin to inquire into the origin of the dramatic luminaries of the first century of the
American theatre you are surprised to find
how many of them were wanderers from
the British Isles; and even within the last
fifty years the record shows a steady and
continuous influx of the dramatic spirit of
the mother-land. Among those actors who
have exercised special influence upon the
American stage since 1750 scarcely more
than a score could be named who were
born in America. With the advent of

Edwin Forrest and Charlotte Cushman the
tide began to turn, and since then the the-
atre in America has expanded and arisen
under the influence of such native-born
Americans as Edwin L. Davenport, Edwin
Booth, William Warren, Joseph Jefferson,
Lawrence Barrett, Lester Wallack, John
Gilbert, Edwin Adams, Genevieve Ward,
Mary Anderson, and Fanny Davenport.
One of the most distinctive products of the
American stage in our generation is Miss
Clara Morris, but Miss Morris was born in
Canada. Ada Rehan, a still more distinctively American product, is a native of
Ireland. She was, however, brought to
America when a child, and in America she
has had her experience and gained her
place. Like many other sparkling persons
born in the land of Goldsmith and Woffington, Miss Rehan has that temperament of
tremulous sensibility which oscillates between smiles and tears ; but, unlike many
of her tumultuous compatriots, she has a
finely balanced mind and that complete
mental control of her faculties and her
artistic resources which is the main constituent of intellectual character. Her performances, therefore, have not only captured the
heart of her time but have convinced its

judgment. They are veritable impersonations, and they are much diversified, but they are strongly marked — as they ought to be — with the individualism of the actor, and this gives to them their chief value. Many actors, like many writers, leave their works, as they pass through the world, much as a carpenter might leave a fabric of his craft that had been purchased from him : the job is done and the goods are delivered. Such actors put nothing of themselves into their art. The product of their effort may be useful, but it is colourless and cold, and no one regards it or remembers it. Ada Rehan has, from the first, been exceptional for intense earnestness and self-devotion. Each part that she has undertaken has been permeated with something of herself, and has been played as well as she could possibly play it. Her soul is given to her profession, and the nature of the woman herself is discerned in that of the character that she represents. Exigent observers of acting have been known to object to that sincerity in an actor, maintaining that the only true actor is he who utterly sinks his identity and comes on so well disguised that he cannot be recognised. That might be a valuable accomplishment in a detective

policeman, but it is a trivial accomplishment in a dramatic artist. The faculty of
taking on many shapes is one of the primi-
tive faculties and it makes a good mimic;
but expertness in the assumption of dis-
guises is not skill in the personification of
character. The interpreter of human nature must go deeper than that. Neither is
it ever desirable that an actor should so far
be obscured in what he represents that his
own spiritual identity, his own personal
quality, shall disappear. The woman who
plays Juliet must represent Juliet's love,
not her own; yet it is with her own voice,
her own eyes, her own demeanour and ways,
that she must represent this, and the passion of her own heart, the glow of her own
spirit, the charm of her own personality,
must enter into the emotion and into the
personality that she assumes to portray.
Murillo painted many contrasted subjects,
but every painting by Murillo bears the
unmistakable stamp of his individualism
and would be worthless without it. A true
actor will show you many different persons,
but in one respect they will be the same —
and ought to be the same — in the pervasive
and dominant attribute of his own genius.
The quality that makes a performance

specifically and distinctively that of Ellen
Terry, or Sarah Bernhardt, or Ada Rehan,
must be present, or the performance may
as well be that of somebody else, — anybody, — a wooden image, for example, that
is worked with strings. Ada Rehan possesses not only the art to personify but the
power to impress herself upon her embodiments; and, therefore, whoever remembers
the matchless figure of Shakespeare's Katharine that she has set upon the stage will
also remember the imperial presence, the
impassioned face, the gray eyes flashing
with pride and scorn or melting with tenderness, the fine freedom of graceful demeanour, the supple beauty of movement
and the exquisite loveliness of voice which
combine in the investiture that the actress
gave to the part, and which are the close
denotements of her own personality.

The characters that have been represented by Ada Rehan since 1874 would
make a long list, and would indicate, as
nothing else can do, the versatility of the
actress, and the drift, variety, and scope of
her study and experience. Resolute, but
not presumptuous courage is one of the
characteristic virtues of that artist, and she
has not hesitated to attempt new characters

or to assume old ones however difficult or however renowned. Her mental attitude is that of a mind that thinks for itself. The veteran actors, indeed, with whom she has been from time to time associated — Edwin Booth, Lawrence Barrett, John McCullough, John T. Raymond, Charles Fisher, Adelaide Neilson, and Mrs. Gilbert — have imparted to her the traditional "business" of many plays. It is in that way that the traditions are preserved. Her manager, Augustin Daly, a close observer and a diligent and practical student of the theatre during many years of active relationship with its affairs, has also aided in her professional education. Many actors receive benefits of that kind, in their upward progress, which some of them are slow to appreciate and quick to forget. Miss Rehan understands them and has been heard to express her sense of their value. Such help has doubtless facilitated her advancement, but in the main her conquest has been due to personal charm, originality of mind, acute and winning sensibility, abundant animal spirits, a gleeful disposition, affluent personal beauty, and the spontaneous custom of looking at character with her own eyes and acting each part in a natural manner. A great merit of the acting of Miss Rehan is its freedom from affectation. Her old-comedy performances have afforded conspicuous illustration of that merit, and of her custom of going directly to the author's text for his meaning and directly to nature for the inspiration of her art. To be simple and natural upon the stage of to-day, in compositions so local and particular as those of Vanbrugh, Wycherley, Cibber, and Farquhar, is not "a property of easiness," yet Miss Rehan has embodied Miss Hoyden, Peggy Thrift, Hippolyta, Sylvia, and Oriana, and she has made those parts appreciable to contemporary intelligence and sympathetic with modern taste. No actress has a happier faculty or a more flexible method of infusing her personal vitality into the old forms. *The Country Wife*, that Wycherley's silken skill embroidered upon the satire of Molière, had to be greatly modified before she could be shown to the fastidious audience of a later day. Garrick converted her into *The Country Girl*, and Augustin Daly refined the texture of the Garrick fabric before introducing her upon the American stage. The result was a pure and deliciously comical image of demurely mischievous girlhood,

and that was personified by Miss Rehan in
a mood of bewitching ingenuousness and
rippling frolic. The ideal is that of an
apparently simple girl, who, in practice of
the harmless wiles of love and courtship,
comically develops a sudden and astonishing dexterity. The mixture of candour and
quaintness in Miss Rehan's manner, giving
zest to exuberant personal charms, invested
that performance with a singular fascination.

In producing those old English comedies
the manager found it essential to alter each
one of them, in some particulars. Advert-
ing to the lax times when they were written, the spectator is not surprised at that
precautionary exercise of prudence and
taste. *The Country Wife* dates back to
1675 ; *The Inconstant*, to 1702 ; *She Would
and She Wouldn't*, to 1703 ; *The Recruiting
Officer*, to 1705, and *The Critic*, to 1781.
In his arrangement of *The Critic* Daly
used many additions that originated with
Charles Mathews, whose incisive, trenchant, sapient impersonation of Mr. Puff
will not be forgotten by any one who had
the privilege of seeing it ; but while *The
Critic*, as Sheridan constructed it, on the
basis of Buckingham's *Rehearsal*, is an

ample three-act piece, Daly's version is
condensed into one act. It was presented
at Daly's theatre on December 26, 1888,
as an afterpiece, and it met with much
favour. Changes in that work are made
merely on the ground of expediency, and
not as a matter of either morality or taste.
It has long been the custom to introduce
local "gags" into *The Critic,* and to vary its
nomenclature, according to the company
that might happen to be representing it.
In that way the apposite significance of the
farce is preserved for each succeeding generation. When the Duke of Buckingham
produced *The Rehearsal* (it was begun in
1663 but was not brought out till 1671), he
directed its chief shaft of satire against
Dryden, who was imaged in the character
of Bayes. When Sheridan produced *The
Critic,* he ridiculed his contemporary Richard Cumberland, who is indicated in Sir
Fretful Plagiary. But no drift of that sort
animates the play for latter times; and in
order that it may be made significant and
piquant to a contemporary audience its satirical mirth is poured upon false methods in
acting as well as upon false taste in composition. The vanity of actors and the
absurd side of stage-tradition are made

ridiculous in it, nor is it devoid of an impli-
cation of satire upon the caprice and the dulness possible to an audience. Miss Rehan, as
Tilburina, proved herself possessed of the
true instinct and faculty of burlesque, for
in the acting of that part she maintained
an air of intense earnestness amounting to
positive solemnity ; she was seemingly both
passionate and pathetic ; and she uttered
the bombastic nonsense of Tilburina's in-
flated speeches with profound and fervid
sincerity.   Her quick lapses from the tragic
manner to that of petulant impatience and
common-place colloquy had an irresistible
effect equally of truth and of involuntary
humour. The faculty that especially ap-
pertains to an actor, that of assuming character and emotion at will, was conspicuously illustrated in that fine performance ;
for in Tilburina's mad-scene — as also in
that of Farquhar's Oriana — Miss Rehan
displayed a degree of feeling and put forth a
quality of power that would be appropriate
and not inadequate even to the delicate,
beautiful, and exacting part of Ophelia.
That is the true way, as Frederick Robson
proved, to play burlesque. It is an old
story that the best comedian is an actor of
deep heart and serious disposition.   When

Miss Rehan embodied M'lle Rose, the Priest's sister, in M. Coppée's striking drama of *The Prayer*, no one acquainted with her nature was surprised at the elemental passion, the pathos, and the almost tragic power with which she expressed a devoted woman's experience of affliction, misery, delirious resentment, self-conquest, self-abnegation, forgiveness, and fortitude. Miss Rehan is not a tragic actress, but she has more power, because deeper feeling, than many serious players of the day, who probably would designate her as gentle and weak. Quin's remark about Mrs. Cibber, when Garrick expressed to him a doubt that she could play Shakespeare's Constance, might well be applied to Miss Rehan : " That woman," he cried, " has a heart and can do anything where passion is required."

Yet it is not distinctively in characters of passion that Miss Rehan has gained her fame. Helena and Katharine, indeed, are passionate persons, but not in the sense in which Constance is passionate, or Juliet, or Queen Margaret, or Otway's Belvidera, or Congreve's Zara. In Helena, who is not less noble than affectionate, the violent infatuation of love for Demetrius, struggling

against self-esteem and prevailing over reticence of character and maidenly reserve,
creates a state of grieved passion not less
afflicting to its victim than touching to her
sympathetic observers. Miss Rehan struck
that note with perfect precision, and it is
seldom that the stage presents such a form
of gentle, forlorn, and winning sweetness
and beauty as the Helena of that actress
was, when seeking to break away from the
wrangle of the lovers in the forest, dejected
and submissive now, asking only that she
may be allowed to go, and saying, in the
soft accents of hopeless sorrow, "You see
how simple and how fond I am." In Katharine the passion is confused; it mingles
many ingredients; but chiefly it is that of
a tumultuous and tempestuous temper. A
strong woman every way, Katharine at first
revolts against every sort of curb or control, and especially against the sweet, loving, ardent impulses inherent in her own
nature. There is tremendous vehemence
in Katharine; but also there is incipient
tenderness, and, therefore, there is self-
conflict; and it was a special and signal
beauty of Miss Rehan's impersonation of
Katharine, that she indicated this by subtle
denotements, and was not merely a whirl-

wind of combative rage. All the passion
that is warranted, or that could be desired,
was expressed; but the crown of the assumption was a woman-like charm, — an ad-
mixture of tremulous sensibility and kind,
caressing, cherishing ardour and goodness;
the something that makes a woman's love
the best blessing that there is in human
life. That attribute, rather than the attribute of passion is the predominant and
distinctive characteristic of Miss Rehan's
dramatic art. No one would expect her to
prosper in the sanguinary queens of the
ancient classic stage, or in the empurpled
criminals of modern melodrama. For such
a nature the Medeas and Phædras, the
Theodoras and Toscas, are out of the question. It is woman in her lovelier aspects
that is portrayed by Miss Rehan; woman
at her best that is suggested by her; and
her success is the more honourable to herself,
and the more beneficent to the public, for
that reason. One of the most womanlike
of all the women that have been drawn in
old comedy is Farquhar's Oriana, and Miss
Rehan's performance of that part was in
her best manner. Oriana is skilful in
coquetry, and she makes a dexterous use of
many wiles in order to subdue and capture

the restless, capricious, vagrant spirit of the
exigent, adventurous, roving Mirabel; but
she dearly loves him, she would die for him,
and she becomes heroic and splendid in his
service, — saving his life by her indomitable
nerve and discreet and expeditious energy.
In male attire, which she assumes in Oriana,
Sylvia, Hippolyta, Peggy Thrift, Viola, and
Rosalind, Miss Rehan is particularly captivating; and, indeed, the spectator is surprised at the number and variety of male
peculiarities that she is able to imitate.
Her assumption of the swaggering gallant,
when Sylvia puts on man's apparel, would
bewitch the sternest judgment, and no one
on the American stage, since the halcyon
days of Mrs. Barrow and Mrs. Wood, has
approximated to her brilliancy of expression
of the gay audacity and elegant insolence
of Hippolyta, when masquerading as Don
Philip, and denouncing him as an impostor, in the home of Don Manuel. Yet, after
all, even in male attire and when meeting
the exigencies of the scene by pretending
to be a man, it is the intrinsic charm of
her womanhood that illumines her art and
invests it with the authentic attribute of
enchantment. That charm is of rare opulence and variety; not readily designated;

not to be put into words; and Miss Rehan's rapid conquest and secure retention
of public favour in the capitals of the new
world and of the old is chiefly explained
by it. When she assumed Rosalind, that
potentiality of personal fascination made
her immediately successful in that character, — of all Shakespeare's women the
one that perhaps is the most readily appreciable, and, at the same time, is the most
frequently in controversy. Her way of acting that part was to be a gleeful yet loving
woman, and not a poetical conceit or a
metaphysical abstraction. Rosalind is not
"of the earth, earthy," but neither is she
made of mist and moonbeams. The blood
dances merrily in her veins, and the fires of
ardent desire equally with the glad lights of
happy mirth sparkle in her eyes. She is a
lover and not ashamed of her love, — which
indeed, like everything else about her, is
natural, simple, spontaneous, and pure. It
is the vain effort to rear upon the basis of
Shakespeare's text, in *As You Like It*, a
superstructure of vague, ethereal, elusive,
strained, complex character and recondite
meaning that has perplexed the stage ideal
of Rosalind and made it seem almost inac-
cessible. But the cloudy refinements that
theory has cast about the part are nowhere

to be found in the play. Miss Rehan's
simple method of treating it was therefore
a great refreshment. She was naturally
noble and free. She made no declaration
of superiority and had no need to announce
that her intentions were virtuous. Her
demeanour showed not the slightest trace of
that self-consciousness which creates indel-
icacy in parts of this order. She was the
image of youth, beauty, happiness, merriment, and of an absorbing and triumphant
love. When she dashed through the trees
of Arden, snatching the verses of Orlando
from their boughs, and cast herself at the
foot of a great elm, to read those fond mes-
sages that Rosalind's heart instantly and
instinctively ascribes to their right source,
her gray eyes were brilliant with tender
joy ; her cheeks were flushed ; her whole
person, in its graceful abandonment of
posture, seemed to express an ecstasy of
happy vitality and of victorious delight ;
her hands that held the written scrolls
trembled with eager, tumultuous, and grateful joy ; the voice with which she read her
lover's words made soft cadences of them
and seemed to caress every syllable ; and
as the last rhyme,

> "Let no face be kept in mind,
> But the fair of Rosalind,"

fell from her lips, like a drop of liquid
silver, the exquisite music of her speech
seemed to die away in one soft sigh of pleasure. While, however, she thus denoted the
passionate heart of Rosalind and her ample
bliss of sensation and exultant yet tender
pride of conquest, she never once relaxed
the tension of her glee. In an ordinary
representation of *As You Like It*, the interest commonly declines after the third
act, if not earlier, from lack of exuberant
physical vitality and of the propulsive force
of sympathetic mirth in Rosalind. When
Ada Rehan played the part the performance
only grew richer and merrier as it proceeded,
— developing the exuberant nature and glad
experience of a loving and enchanting
woman who sees the whole world suffused
with golden light, irradiated from her own
happy heart, her healthful and brilliant
mind, her buoyant spirit and inexhaustible
goodness and joy.

There are many actors of whom the play-
goer thinks with interest and mild approbation, but it is only of the few that he thinks
with enthusiasm. Ada Rehan is one of the
few, and always the mention of her name
awakens a thrill of sympathy. Beauty,
genius, a kind heart, and rare technical

skill — things seldom united in one person
— are united in her, and those attributes, in
their union, constitute a power such as must
always play a serious part in human affairs.
Practical minds may despise and contemn
the idea of sentiment as to an actress ; but
each succeeding generation of youth has
its heroines of the stage, who exert upon it,
at the most sensitive and susceptible period
of life, — colouring its ideals, affecting its
ambitions, and aiding to form its character,
— an influence both profound and permanent. Anne Bracegirdle possessed a prodigious power of that kind, in her day, and
so, at a later time, did Peg Woffington, and
Sarah Siddons, and Dora Jordan, and Ellen
Tree, and Adelaide Neilson. There is
scarcely a memoir of a distinguished man
within the last hundred years that does not
show him, at an early, and sometimes at a
late period of his career, in subservience to
the spell of genius and art diffused from the
stage by a beautiful woman. Even so great
a man as Matthew Arnold has recorded that
he followed from city to city in order to see
Rachel. How essential it is that this artistic
influence should be noble every thinker will
at once feel and concede, for its consequences are momentous and endless. The

time is blessed beyond its knowledge of its
own welfare that is favoured with such an
actress as Ada Rehan. If thirty years had
passed away and she had become a memory
instead of being what she now is, a lovely
and beneficent presence, there would be no
reluctance in the general admission of the
truth. The word that then would be said
with pensive regret may now, accordingly,
be said with grateful admiration. For the
people of her own generation this actress
is a representative image and an authentic
voice. Her experience becomes to some
extent their experience, and her testimony
as to each elemental impulse and feeling
of human nature, transmitted through the
potencies of dramatic art, largely contributes
to shape their views and establish their convictions. For many a day the standard of
dramatic art that she has erected in Shakespeare's Rosalind and in Farquhar's Oriana,
in Lady Teazle and Letitia Hardy, will maintain itself with inexorable authority upon
the stage, while the ideals of passionate and
tender womanhood that she has embodied
in such characters as Katharine, Helena
and Viola, Sister Rose and Kate Verity
and Knowles's Julia will crystallise in the
popular imagination and enkindle and
charm the popular heart.

Another Shakespearian character in which the subject of this essay proved proficient and charming is Mrs. Ford, in *The Merry Wives of Windsor*. That piece, among Shakespeare's comedies, is perhaps the most modern and contemporaneous. In that play a couple of sprightly women undertake and accomplish the discomfiture of a vicious, presumptuous, ridiculous suitor. Such a frolic might be possible at any time and in any place. The two wives, Mrs. Ford and Mrs. Page, are virtuous women, but they are not fastidious. Mrs. Ford is a ripe, buxom, captivating woman, overflowing with animal spirits and fond of innocent mischief, — in the expedients of which she is fertile and dexterous. She looks upon the amorous Falstaff with amused tolerance which scarcely amounts to contempt. She will thoroughly fool and rebuke him, and will throw him aside with precisely the sort of punishment that will plunge him into absurdity and humiliation. But she is not malicious, neither does she harbour resentment. The right personification of Mrs. Ford involves innate purity and spontaneous, unequivocal moral worth, combined with a buoyant spirit of frolicsome mischief, and an arch, demure,

piquant manner. Miss Rehan entered fully
into the spirit of the part and flashed
through the piece like a sunbeam. The
reality of that embodiment was especially
vital. In Mrs. Ford, as in Sylvia, Miss
Rehan presented a woman in whom an exuberant and sportive animal life transcends
all other attributes. And, indeed, one way
or another, subject to various modifications,
that element enters into all of her comedy
assumptions, particularly the blooming
damsels and spirited widows of the comedy
of to-day. Doris, in *An International
Match*, and Nisbe, in *A Night Off*, are good
types of the eager, sprightly, happy girl
whom she portrays with infectious buoyancy and in the spontaneous, flexible, limpid drift of nature. Cousin Val, — Valentine Osprey, — in *The Railroad of Love*,
embodies that personality in even a more
substantial form, and interfuses it with
passionate emotion. In Nisbe there is latent mischief commingled with an artful
assumption of girlish coyness. In Cousin
Val, a deep heart is veiled beneath an
almost reckless gayety of manner, and
much tenderness of feeling becomes visible
through an outward guise of raillery and
gleeful indifference. Miss Rehan's expres-

sion of the resentment of offended pride
and wounded love, in the scene of the mis-
understanding in that piece, is remembered
for its splendid sincerity, its fine fervour,
and its absolute simplicity of art. The play
treats of an impending breach between two
sincere lovers and of the happy chance by
which that catastrophe was averted. An
impulsive woman, momentarily persuaded
that her suitor is a mercenary adventurer,
has sent a harsh letter of dismissal to him,
and then has ascertained that her doubt
was unfounded and unworthy ; whereupon
she perceives the imperative necessity that
her letter, which by chance has not reached
him, should be recovered. Her plan is to
detain him during her quest for that dreaded
epistle, which she will obtain and destroy,
so that he may never know how unjust and
how cruel her thoughts have been. The
structure of the situation rests on unwar-
ranted panic, — since Valentine might take
for granted her lover's pardon, — but the
situation itself is fraught with formidable
significance and suffused with passionate
excitement. Miss Rehan made it important and impressive. Her denotement of
the conflict of passion, when writing the
letter, lifted Valentine quite to the high

level of Julia in a kindred passage in *The
Hunchback,* while her subsequent contrition and dismay, her effort to subdue a
feverish apprehension, and to conceal her
anxiety under a playful manner, together
with her grieved yet gay trepidation while
imposing upon her lover the frivolous task
of doing a bit of embroidery, were all made
confluent in a current of singular sweetness
and were swathed in the tremulous April
atmosphere of smiles and tears. Altogether
that assumption of character, not inapt-
ly representative of contemporary young
women, in the sentimental aspect of their
lives, was remarkable equally for the variety and sparkle of its constituent parts
and for the mingled force and piquancy of
its art; for it was an image of airy banter,
satirical raillery, piquant archness, demure
mischief, pungent sarcasm, irrational, tan-
talising, delicious feminine caprice, nobility
of mind, and passionate ardour of heart.
In the centuries that have passed since the
drama began to bear witness to human nature and social life, woman has been the
same creature of infinite variety and often
inexplicable complexity, herself creative
and therefore unconsciously participant in
the insoluble mystery of creation; but in

each succeeding period woman has existed
as a social type with distinguishing traits
and characteristics. In the present period
she conspicuously shows the attributes that
crystallised in Miss Rehan's embodiment of maids like Doris and dames like
Valentine. The heroines of modern comedy are seen to act from the same motives
and to pursue the same objects that impel
and attract the heroines of Cibber, Farquhar, Mrs. Centlivre, Mrs. Inchbald, and
Sheridan; yet they are essentially of a
different order of thought and manner.
The heroine of to-day does not pique her
roving swain by getting into male attire and
facing him down as an impostor; neither
does she pretend to be a piteous lunatic in
order to lure him out of his intrenchments;
but she loves as dearly, she is just as expert, whether in hiding her love or in showing it, she is just as wishful to captivate,
and she is just as fitful and capricious, as
any Hippolyta, or Oriana, or Sylvia, or
Mrs. Sullen, or Violante, or Lydia Lan-
guish, that ever sparkled on the remote
British stage.

The successful stage representative of
woman proves true to the specific character
of her time as well as to the elemental and

permanent character of her sex. She does
not live in the study but in the world. Her
works are personifications and not historical antiquities. Miss Rehan might not succeed in reproducing such fantastic women
as often were drawn by Jonson and Dryden, but any woman of the old comedy
who is really a woman would become as
vital and sympathetic in her embodiment
as if she were living in the actual world of
to-day. It is for the lecturer to expound;
it is for the actor to interpret. Miss Rehan,
like her great and renowned sister in dramatic art, Ellen Terry, — the most distinctively poetic actress of this century, in any
language, or in any land, — possesses the
power to personify and can give the touch
of reality. The young women of to-day
see themselves in Ada Rehan's portrayals
of them. The young men of to-day recognise in those portrayals the fulfilment of
that ideal of sensuous sentiment, piquant
freedom, and impetuous ardour, combined
with rich beauty of person and negligent
elegance of manner, which they account
the perfection of womanhood, and upon
which their fancy dwells with supreme content. That this lovely actress can move
easily in the realm of the imagination is

proved by her fluent and sparkling performances of Rosalind and Viola ; but it is more
significant, for the great body of contemporary play-goers, that she can speak in the
voice, and look through the eyes, and interpret the spirit, of the passing hour.

Among the incidental yet notable performances that have been given by Miss Rehan
there are two which strongly suggested
her exceptional versatility. One of these
is Xantippe, in *The Wife of Socrates ;* the
other is Jenny O'Jones, in *Red-Letter
Nights.* The first of those pieces is a bit
of blank-verse dialogue, written by Mr.
Justin H. McCarthy, upon the basis of a
French piece by M. Theodore de Banville.
It was produced at Daly's theatre on October 30, 1888. Miss Rehan wore a robe of
golden silk and her noble and spirited head
was crowned with an aureole of red hair.
Xantippe, resentful of the perfect composure of Socrates, scolds and storms till, in
the tempest of her passion she is suddenly
thrown into a syncope, whereupon she is
thought to be dead. But while she is re-
covering from that swoon she hears the sorrowful, affectionate protestations of love that
are uttered by her husband, and perceiving
then his sincerity, devotion, and sweetness,

and her own unwomanlike violence and acrimony of temper, she changes from a shrew
to a meek and loving woman. Miss Rehan
acted that part in a strain of passionate
impetuosity, and, at times, with fine sarcasm. Her elocution was uncommonly
sweet. Her action was marked by incessant and piquant variety. She flashed from
one mood to another, and placed many
phases of the feminine nature in vivid contrast. The embodiment was one of sumptuous personal beauty, and after the storm
of shrewish rage and turbulent jealousy had
spent its force, the portrayal closed with the
suggestion of a lovely ideal of nobility and
gentleness. When there is a close correspondence between the temperament of the
actor and the temperament of the part that
is represented a greater freedom of expression is naturally reached. That correspondence existed in the culminating passage of
that play, between Miss Rehan and the
conquered Xantippe ; and her success was
triumphant. In dealing with the shrewish
aspect of the part she obeyed the same
subtle impulse that she had wisely followed
in her treatment of Shakespeare's Katharine : the dress was made to harmonise with
the spirit of its wearer. Her shrew was red-

haired, high-coloured, and like a scorching flame. Set against that brilliant embodiment Jenny O'Jones, which is a farcical episode, inspired a sentiment of wonder that the same woman should be able to invest with a suitable body two such utterly divergent and contrasted souls. The character was made by Daly and written by him into his version of a German play, which he named *Red-Letter Nights*. In that scene Miss Rehan, representing an amiable though wild and mischievous girl, was constrained to adopt the same expedient that Letitia Hardy chooses, in *The Belle's Stratagem*, though with a different purpose. Being sought in marriage by a disagreeable old man, the heroine pretends to be a slatternly hoiden, and her singing of a song, about Jenny O'Jones, which she declares to contain more than a hundred verses, all of which are alike, discomfits the obnoxious applicant and puts him to flight. It is a violent expedient of humour, —it is much as if Rosalind should pretend to be Audrey, — but it is exceedingly droll, and, seeing that the actress whose art can touch such extremes of character and of poetry as Katharine and Rosalind, Ophelia and Peggy Thrift, Julia and Marian Lea, can also create and sustain an illusion in the domain of downright broad farce, the observer is naturally impressed by that rare and fine capacity which distinctively marks an actor, — the capacity of impersonation. It is that faculty, authenticated and made irresistible by personal charm, that has made Ada Rehan a leader in her profession, and has prompted this tribute to the grace, humour, tenderness, and beauty of her acting, and to the auspicious worth of her artistic powers.

And that point contains the sum of thoughts that are prompted by the subject. It is a common opinion, and sometimes it finds expression, that any person who is self-possessed, and is able to deliver language in an effective manner, is, therefore, able to act. There could not be a greater delusion. Self-possession in the presence of an audience, which obviously is essential, comes by experience ; but elocution will not make an actor. It is a useful and a charming accomplishment, but in the art of acting it is of secondary importance. The first qualification for an actor must always be the faculty of getting inside of a character, giving to it a body, and presenting it as a truth. Miss Rehan is excellent, even

among the best, as a speaker of English,
whether verse or prose ; yet, though her
elocution were defective, her distinguishing
dramatic ability would remain unimpaired.
Just as, in a dramatic composition, the
quality that makes it a play and not a narrative is a quality neither literary nor phi-
osophical, neither analytical nor poetic, so
in a dramatic performer the quality that
makes the actor is neither scholarship, nor
logic, nor eloquence, nor ingenuity, but a
certain power of being something and doing
something, which converts words into actions, and constructs before the eyes of the
spectator a moving picture of human life,
with its background of materialism and its
atmosphere of spiritual mystery. That
power of being and doing is the soul of the
stage. Those persons who possess it, and
those alone, touch the heart, arouse the
imagination, and justify and dignify and
advance the profession of the actor. In
that large body of writing which is called
dramatic criticism, and which has been
created and copiously augmented by the
futile literary industry of more than two
hundred years, it is astonishing to observe
how little thought the reader is able to discover that goes to the question of what the

actor does and of how he does it. For one
page about what Garrick actually did, in
any one of Shakespeare's characters, you
may find a hundred about what Shakespeare possibly meant. For one writer
like Cibber or Tom Davies, who tells you
much, you may find fifty like Tom Brown
and Anthony Pasquin, who tell you nothing. Yet were it not for what the actor
contributes — investing with a body that
soul which the author has conceived, — the
part of wisdom would be to stay at home
and read the play in peace, at a comfortable
fireside. It is that which makes certain
men and women great in what were else
an idle mimicry of serious and substantial
things, and it is because they are great, in
the possession and exercise of that power,
that the study of their witchcraft is worthy
of intellectual attention while it is at hand,
and worthy to be seized and commemorated
if possible, before it drifts away. In the
presence of such women as Ellen Terry and
Ada Rehan, — the representative actresses
of England and America, — Tyndall, with
all his learning, Gladstone, with all his eloquence, Tennyson, with all his poetic genius,
subside to a second place in immediate popular interest. That may be strange, but it

is true ; and it would cease to be strange if
the character, methods, and purpose of the
dramatic faculty, together with the enchantment which invests a beautiful woman
to whom nature has given it, were more
intelligently studied and better understood.

" Num tu, quæ tenuit dives Achæmenes
    Aut pinguis Phrygiæ Mygdonias opes
Permutare velis crine Licymniæ,
    Plenas aut Arabum domos ? —
Dum flagrantia detorquet ad oscula
Cervicem, aut facili sæivita negat,
    Quæ poscente magis gaudeat eripi,
    Interdum rapere occupet."

XIX.

THE STORY OF ADELAIDE NEILSON.

1846 (?) — 1880.

IT may have been with a premonition of
the bereavement which was at hand that
the present writer endeavoured, during
Adelaide Neilson's last season in America,
to make something like an adequate estimate of her genius and of the worth and
beauty of her art. It certainly was with
knowledge of the strain to which she was
subjected, and the serious danger — a tendency to neuralgia of the heart — which,
in her unsparing and incessant professional
exertions, she frequently incurred. It also
was with the conviction that — within a certain line of character — she was the best
actress of this epoch, and that she would
be seen here no more. There is a kind of
satisfaction in the remembrance that the
tribute then paid to her, in earnestness
alike of thought and feeling, was, at least
in purpose, such as her fine powers and

achievements deserved, and such as carried to her kind and sensitive heart a sense of comfort. It is not easily possible to define the charm of that extraordinary person. Her death gave the privilege of unreserved comment upon her goodness as well as her genius.

Miss Neilson ended her engagement at Booth's theatre on May 24, 1880, and started the next day for San Francisco, where she acted from June 8 till July 13. She then returned to New York and on July 28 sailed, aboard the Abyssinia, for England. Eighteen days afterwards she was dead — in her youth and beauty, in the ripeness of her fame, at the end of great toils, and just in the morning of what was hoped would be a new life of happiness and peace. Never was a more brilliant career arrested in its meridian by a more sudden stroke of fate. Never did death seem more untimely or loss more irreparable. For many a day the stage, bereft of her radiant presence, seemed desolate; and to persons who knew her well and saw the loveliness of her disposition, the gentleness of her spirit, the large generosity of her mind, and the radiance of cheerfulness that she diffused, the life of the stage will not again be as bright as once it was.

Adelaide Neilson was about thirty-four years old when she died. She had been on the stage fifteen years and she often said that her novitiate was full of hardship. Her last birthday she passed in New York, at the Westminster hotel, and she was then looking forward hopefully to the success of her farewell engagements and to tranquil days in retirement in her cherished home in England. Whatever may have been the vicissitudes, trials, errors, and sorrows of her past, she was by nature a woman of domestic tastes — affectionate, gentle, confiding; and she would have made her home happy.

A record of much labour and many successes, on the London stage and all over Great Britain, and of four visits to America is her brief biography. It will not be amiss to note, with some emphasis, the fact of her youth as it is seen when coupled with such abundant achievement. She was, to have done so much, a very young woman. She was in that sense a prodigy — and it is remarkable that she bore so well the always perilous burdens of early triumph. She had the intuitions of genius and also its quick spirit and wild temperament. She was largely ruled by her imagination and her feelings, and had neither the prudence of selfishness nor the craft of experience. Such a nature might easily go to shipwreck and ruin. She outrode the storms of a passionate, wayward youth and anchored safe at last in the haven of duty. Her image, as it rises in memory, is not that of the actress who stormed the citadel of all hearts in the delirium of Juliet, or dazzled with the witchery of Rosalind's glee or Viola's tender grace; but it is that of the grave, sweet woman, who, playing softly in the twilight, sang — in a rich, tremulous, touching voice — the anthem on the man of sorrows acquainted with grief.

It may be she did not die too soon for her fame. The work had been done that it was appointed for her to do. No shaft of malice or envy can ever wound again that gentle heart. No word of detraction can sully the white roses of pity that cover her blameless dust. For herself all is well; but for the world she sleeps too early and too long.

"Here's a few flowers; but about midnight
    more:
The herbs that have on them cold dew o' the
    night
Are strewings fitt'st for graves."

The story of Adelaide Neilson's life is
largely a story of hardship and sorrow.
She was born out of wedlock, in or near
Leeds, Yorkshire, England, on March 3, in
(probably) 1846. Her father's name is unknown. Her mother, an actress, was Miss
Browne — who subsequently became Mrs.
Bland. As a child Adelaide lived at Skip-
ton and subsequently at the village of
Guiseley, near Leeds, where she was reared
in humble circumstances and where she
worked in a factory. She was a pretty
and precocious child, skilful with her
needle and fond of reading. Before she
was twelve years old she had become acquainted with many plays and in particular
with some of the tragedies of Shakespeare.
She read her mother's play-books — relics
of the profession that Miss Browne had left
— and it was her childish custom to act and
declaim before an audience of dolls that she
herself had made. She sometimes witnessed
dramatic performances given in the neighbourhood by strolling players. She attended the parochial school at Guiseley,
and her teacher Mr. Frizell remembers her
as an attentive, studious pupil, possessed
of a good memory and an unusual talent
for recitation. She was an attendant at the

Methodist church also, and she is remembered in her youthful home as an industrious and unselfish girl, docile, gentle, considerate, ready to do any work that came to her hand, and although consciously beautiful neither spoiled by vanity nor embittered by coarse surroundings and hard usage.

When she was about fourteen years old she discovered by accident the secret of her birth and after that time she became discontented and restless. There never had been sympathy between the mother and the child, and after that discovery Adelaide went out to service as a nurse-maid, and in that employment she continued for about two years, when she determined to leave Guiseley and seek her fortune in London. She was then in her seventeenth year, and was known by the name of Lizzie Ann Bland. She left her home secretly and proceeded first to Leeds and afterwards to London. She was destitute and friendless and during the next three years she led a hard life and met with wretched experiences. At length she obtained employment in the theatre, and little by little she made her way to a position of some influence. Her first important professional appearance was made in 1865 at Margate, where she enacted Juliet. The name that she adopted soon after she went to London was Lilian Adelaide Lessont — which afterwards was changed to Neilson ; and at the time of her first appearance a romantic story was circulated, to the effect that she was the daughter of a Spanish nobleman and an English governess and that her birthplace was Saragossa. That fiction clung to her for a long time.

Her first appearance in London was made, in the summer of 1865, at the Royalty theatre, in the character of Juliet. She subsequently appeared as Gabrielle De Savigny in *The Huguenot Captain*. A little later she was at the Adelphi theatre, where she played Victorine in the drama of that name. For several years she made a hard struggle for a high position and her career was full of vicissitude. Among the parts that she played were Nelly Armroyd in *Lost in London*, Lilian in *Life for Life*, Mary Belton in *Uncle Dick's Darling*, and Madame Vidal in *A Life Chase*. She also appeared in *Stage and State* and in *The Captain of the Vul-*

ture, and in 1870, as Amy Robsart, she made a conspicuous hit, at Drury Lane. On December 19, 1870, she acted at that theatre as Juliet, and then she created an impression that was destined to endure. She had in the course of those preliminary years made several tours of the British provincial cities and in particular had amazed the inhabitants of Leeds and of her native place. She had also become the wife of Mr. Philip Lee, the son of a clergyman at Stoke Bruerne, Northamptonshire, from whom, however, she was divorced in 1877. In 1872, accompanied by Mr. Lee, she made her first visit to America, appearing first at Booth's theatre as Juliet. She revisited America in 1874, 1876, and 1879.

In the summer of 1880, when Miss Neilson had taken her farewell of the American stage and sailed for Europe, she intended to pass a considerable time in retirement and repose. She was broken in health and much more broken in spirit — although in outward appearance as well as and as beautiful as ever. She died suddenly at Paris, on August 15, 1880, and her body was brought to London and buried in Brompton Cemetery. A white marble cross marks

her grave, inscribed with the words "Gifted
and Beautiful — Resting." [1]

[1] A letter to me from London, dated August 20,
1880, gives a glimpse of her funeral:

"I have just come from Brompton Cemetery
where the funeral took place at noon. The sky was
clouded all the morning and there was a light rain
just before the hearse and carriages arrived, but the
sun came out, and it was quite warm as the services
were held at the grave. There was such a concourse
of people that the mourners were almost mobbed.
It was decided to follow the hearse to the grave on
foot from the chapel instead of going in the carriages,
but this was to be regretted, for the crowd was so
dense and so unruly that those who felt the solemnity of the scene, and had a right to follow all that
remained of our poor friend, were pushed and hustled
and, in some instances, kept back altogether from
the grave. After brief services in the chapel the
coffin (which was of light wood, with an inscribed
silver plate, and was covered with a wreath and two
crosses of white flowers and geranium leaves) was
again placed in the great hearse, drawn by four
plumed horses. The mourners followed on foot,
and all the way to the grave the chapel bell tolled
solemnly. Admiral Glyn and Lady Sinclair, E.
Compton, Mrs. John Wood, and Miss Fanny Josephs
were among the mourners. I saw there Miss Car-
lotta Leclercq (Mrs. Nelson), in widow's weeds and
bearing a white wreath, John S. Clarke, and Miss
Helen Barry. The narrow vault was lined with
purple and the white flowers were left on the coffin.
It is such a dreadfully sudden bereavement that
everyone here who knew her is stunned by it. She
had a very lovely nature."

XX.

HENRY IRVING AND ELLEN TERRY IN
MACBETH.

ON September 18, 1875, at the Lyceum theatre in London, Henry Irving appeared as Macbeth for the first time. He had not yet assumed the management of that theatre, but he had gained his great success there in Hamlet, having played that part for two hundred consecutive nights, and he was in the flood-tide of public favour; so that whatever he might do was sure to be regarded with respect and interest. He acted Macbeth for eighty nights, and he revived it for six weeks on December 16, 1876. After that he left it untouched for twelve years, when he again presented it, and with such magnificence of environment as never was lavished on it before. That revival was accomplished on December 29, 1888. Macbeth was played by Irving; Lady Macbeth by Ellen Terry.

No actor troubles the waters so much as Henry Irving does. The strength of his character, the originality of his mind, the resolute persistency of his purpose, the charm of his temperament, and the great vitality of his conduct unite to make him an extraordinary figure and a potent force in the world of art and in the cultured circles of society. His appearance in any character is a signal for division of opinion. His appearance as Macbeth started a critical controversy, and the dispute still rages. His advocates hail the embodiment of Macbeth as a conspicuous illustration of the beauty and felicity of method with which he invests an ideal creation with the attributes of humanity and thus interprets the Shakespearian original, not as a poetic abstraction or a stage figure, but as an actual, possible, and comprehensible human being. His assailants, on the contrary, while they concede that his acting is at times magnificent, declare that he has misunderstood the drift of the tragedy, and that the ideal of Macbeth presented by him is false. The historical accuracy of scenes and dresses, the copious variety of embellishment, the felicitous adjuncts, and in general the weird splendour with which he produced the tragedy were admitted on every hand, and were not only admitted, but warmly extolled.

Henry Irving apprehends Macbeth from a point of view that no other actor or student of the part has taken. He insists that a man capable of such damnable treachery and such horrible crimes can never have had any good in him; that Macbeth is radically wicked. He perceives that Macbeth suffers from remorse, or from something like it, but he perceives that this suffering precedes as well as follows the murder of Duncan, and therefore, and for other reasons, he concludes that the sensibility of Macbeth is not moral but poetical, meaning thereby that it is unreal. According to that view the real Macbeth is to be sought, not in his words, but exclusively in his deeds. He intends from the first to murder the king, to murder the prince of Cumberland, to murder Banquo, to murder anybody and everybody who stands between his ambition and the Scottish throne. It was he who first conceived the plan of killing Duncan, and broke that enterprise to his wife by letter — not by any means a new doctrine. Once entered on his career of assassin and butcher he stops at nothing. He is wading in blood, and it were as tedious to turn back as to proceed. He will slaughter even the little children of his adversary —

"his wife, his babes, and all unfortunate souls that trace him in his line." Yet all the while he is in misery, because all the while his fine poetic intuition, his imaginative grasp of life and of its mysterious and sublime environments, make him acutely aware of the enormity of his conduct, the consequences, both horrible and pathetic, of his dastardly deeds, "the pity of it," and the utter emptiness of all that he has gained. In other words, Macbeth is a ruffian who halts at no crime for the accomplishment of his purpose, but who is continually avenged upon himself through the excess of his poetic sensibility. Another man would suffer through conscience; Macbeth suffers through imagination. That, clearly, was Irving's position. He cannot accept the old doctrine of Macbeth's original virtue and inherent nobleness, because to him it seems preposterous and incredible that a virtuous and noble person should steal upon his sleeping guest at a midnight hour and stab him to death in his bed. But in practical effect as to the performance of the part it would not appear to make any difference whether Macbeth suffers from the stings of conscience or the stings of imagination, so that he suffers.

Irving in fact acted Macbeth in a spirit of subtle sympathy with the poetry of Shakespeare's conception, albeit with some deficiency of robust and massive physique, and with some excess of metaphysical analysis. The commotion created by his performance among critics of the drama was due in a far greater degree to what he said or caused to be said about Macbeth than to anything that he did in playing it. He disappointed the conventional view of Macbeth, which insists on his being a Hercules ; but since his Macbeth was almost effeminate, in lack of moral courage and in frequent moments of terror-stricken collapse, he did not disappoint thoughtful judges of the dramatic art. A performance as it is may differ very widely from a performance as it seems to be, in the hair-splitting analysis of an ideal on paper. Mrs. Siddons was great in Lady Macbeth, but her essay on the character is not deemed indicative of her greatness in it. The figure of Irving's Macbeth in his gold armour was a thrilling presence, and his desperate fight at the last was a tremendous spectacle of delirious valour.

With the old theory of Macbeth most readers are familiar. He is, at the outset, a heroic soldier, "Bellona's bridegroom," "worthy Macbeth." But there is a germ of evil in him, and the forces of evil that besiege the world — embodied and indicated by the three witches — are enabled to obtain possession of him. "Something wicked this way comes." Both Macbeth and his wife are dominated by fiends. Both are wicked, but the man is weaker in his wickedness than the woman, because prescient, imaginative, and even tender, and therefore he is the more ruthless and bloody. Remorse and fear, reacting on a courageous nature, drive it into an insane fury, and that is mostly the condition of Macbeth. The pathos of the tragedy arises from the utter inability of those doomed creatures to escape their terrible destiny of evil. Their loneliness upon the barren eminence of sin to which they have mounted almost breaks the heart to witness. Nothing in literature is more touching than the cold and solitary anguish of those two ravaged figures standing together in the deserted and silent banquet-room after the scene of Banquo's ghost. When Macbeth and his Queen are acted in the spirit indicated by those views, the tragedy is made no less significant to the heart than impressive to the imagination. That great actress Charlotte Cushman declared that Macbeth is the great-grandfather of all the Bowery ruffians; but that is a mistake. He loses all grandeur and all sympathy, and furthermore all interest, when he is presented in that guise.

Ellen Terry as Lady Macbeth was both awful and pathetic. Those actors who grasp a character by intuition are always better than those who think their way to it, and Ellen Terry is strong in her intuitions. The ideal of Lady Macbeth that she presented is that of the fragile, fascinating woman, not the masculine termagant. Mrs. Siddons thought that Lady Macbeth should be slender and delicate, full of fire and spirit, but exquisitely feminine. It is certain that Macbeth loves her. A minute, profound, and truthful exposition of that aspect of the subject was never given upon the stage until Ellen Terry gave it. Shakespeare did not leave it out of his scheme. No man is any longer a mystery when you know the woman who is in his heart. Ellen Terry made Lady Macbeth a ruler of her husband through his love for her, and not through her superior force of character or her insensibility to danger,

horror, or sin. And she depicted with
heart-breaking fidelity to nature the hopeless remorse — which is not contrition —
the desolate blank of silent, corroding
misery, with no possibility of repentance
or relief, and no fear of the future, because
nothing can be more terrible and afflicting
than the present — under which the frail
body of the queen weakens, till at last,
"by self and violent hands," she puts a
period to her mortal woe and sleeps forever.

XXI.

IRVING AND COQUELIN.

IT is manifestly indecorous for one artist to publish adverse criticism of another. M. Coquelin's paper on *Acting and Actors*, published in *Harper's Magazine*, for May, 1887, while it contained instructive and suggestive observation, presented an example of that blemish — for it referred, by name, to Henry Irving, and it disparaged his method of acting. Irving, who has endured, from legitimate sources, more adverse criticism than any other actor now living, and that without injury to either his reputation or temper, naturally viewed with disapproval the strictures upon his person and his art put forth by another actor, and thereupon he answered M. Coquelin, one month later, with an article in *The Nineteenth Century*. The two papers suggest a comprehensive and lucid summary of the philosophy of the dramatic art.

"Criticism," says Irving, "is generally sufficient in the hands of the professors

of the art ; but when an actor takes up its
functions, for the enlightenment of other
actors, and, with the freedom of M.
Coquelin, invites comparisons and suggests
parallels, he runs no little risk of a grave
misapprehension of his purpose. If every
artist were to rush into print with his opinions of his compeers there would be a disagreeable rise in the social temperature."
In those moderate but pungent words
Irving signified his sense of the French
comedian's ungracious personal reference.
He was entirely in the right ; and, furthermore, it was found, in a studious perusal
of both those papers, that while on several
points the two actors are accordant, at
every point where there is divergence of
opinion Irving had largely the advantage.

The divergences of opinion relate mainly
to the essence of natural acting and of
poetical tragedy. What constitutes " natural " acting, and what share shall be per-
mitted to what is called " the ideal " in
dramatic art ? M. Coquelin, as those observers who have seen and studied his acting might naturally expect, attaches much
importance to variety of physical investiture and to photographic fidelity of detail.
His essay, as Irving has not omitted to

remark, "contains a comforting proportion of truisms" and "frequently upsets in one paragraph the proposition of another." "Always merge your individuality" is the doctrine with which he begins, and "never set aside your individuality" is the doctrine with which he ends. But so far as he has succeeded in making his meaning obvious —in rather a diffuse and tangled piece of writing — he would have the actor invent a new, separate, and distinct physical investiture for each character that he assumes. The actor's identity must disappear. The actor's feelings must never be real. The actor's inner consciousness and intellectual purpose must watch over and direct and control the actor's exterior machinery. The actor must always keep inside of the character. The actor who has the command of many parts is superior to the actor who can command but one. Granted. Twice two is four. But all are aware, who have observed the stage, that there never yet was an actor (certainly M. Coquelin is no exception to the rule), who could divest his work of the idiosyncrasy of his nature; that it makes no difference whether the actor's feelings are real or unreal, as long as he holds them in perfect control and produces the

effect of aroused emotion in others; and
that, as a matter of experience, every actor,
no matter how much cleverness he may
show in getting creditably through a great
number of parts, eventually finds his range
limited to three or four characters; and
those in the line of his own most salient
and essential attributes. Just as a Murillo
or a Rembrandt, painting many subjects,
nevertheless leaves upon each and every
work a personal impress and character —
which is the touch of the master, and for
which the work is valued — so will a Kean,
a Kemble, a Coquelin, an Irving, a Booth,
a Jefferson, or a Salvini, playing different parts, invest each one with an invariable personality. As to the rest, you
have only to consult your recollections of
such actors as Forrest, Burton, Warren,
Owens, Gilbert, Wallack, and Blake. They
played many parts; but how few are the
parts in which they are remembered because great! No human being can escape
from himself.

M. Coquelin said that Irving is an actor
who never clothes himself with the semblance of a character but always clothes
the character with his own semblance. In
that his misapprehension of the English

actor ran to the verge of injustice. The more important because radical defect of M. Coquelin's reasoning was its prosaic blindness to the ideal. Fortunately he is a better actor than he seems to be in his writings. "He completely misses," says Irving, "the vital essence of tragedy; his criticism is of the earth earthy." That comment was perfectly justified. But it ought to be remembered that of what English and American people mean by "poetry" the French have not the slightest gleam of apprehension. Shakespeare, to a Frenchman, does not exist. There was once a French critic who much admired what he called Shakespeare's accuracy of description, in *Macbeth*, of the climate of Scotland — as being "Hail, Hail! All Hail!" That is not a bad hint of the way in which the French appreciate "The Divine Williams."

The statement has been persistently made, and for so long a time that at last it has acquired the authority of longevity, that French dramatic ideas and French actors are invariably and necessarily better than English ideas and English actors. That, however, is not the truth. The art of tragic acting, as our people understand it, is unknown to the French stage. The

French actors, when good ones, excel in comedy; but many French actors are tedious because they belittle great subjects by a petty treatment of them, and because they place inordinate stress upon trifling details and call it "nature." Sarah Bernhardt, who is accounted the best of French players, has failed — although an expert executant — in every noble part that ever she undertook to act. Charles Fetcher, certainly a fine artist, when he came to the graveyard scene in *Hamlet*, used to sit on a tomb and cross his legs and nurse his boot, with the nonchalant familiarity of a Robert Macaire. The French actors are fine photographers — and there, for the most part, they stop. A mercurial temperament, like the Gallic, naturally expresses itself in effusive movement and gesticulation. The English temperament, which is deep, passionate, and of a composite order, containing many latent qualities, inclines to gravity and reticence in ordinary life; but, when it does liberate itself into expression, it moves and speaks with a hundred times the celerity, vigor, and intensity of the more volatile and superficial races. The French have never produced such a poet as Byron, such a cap-

tain as Nelson, such a statesman as Pitt,
such an orator as Fox, or such actors as
Garrick, Mrs. Siddons, Edmund Kean,
Ellen Terry, and Henry Irving. In acting
the Irish have achieved greater things than
the French — their record in the dramatic
field being exceptionally brilliant. But
Garrick, in his day, predominated over his
Irish rivals, — hard-driven though he may
have been by both Henderson and Barry;
and Kean, in his day, eclipsed everybody
on the stage. The French sometimes produce a genius, like Rachel, who shatters
their total fabric of lace and embroidery;
but the essential greatness of achievement
in the dramatic art is found in the record
of the English stage. It is a stultifying delusion that the votary of acting is bound to
worship everything dramatic that comes out
of France.

XXII.

WILLARD AS JOHN NEEDHAM.

IN dealing, for a dramatic result, with the
evil deeds of man, the dramatist may
probe and portray the human nature of the
criminal, as Shakespeare did in the stupen-
dous tragedy of *Macbeth*, or he may concentrate his art upon situation, and content
himself with depicting the manner and the
details of the crime. In the former case
his play will possess imaginative and psy-
chical interest, and will diffuse a spectator's
thoughts over the whole broad subject of
good and evil. In the latter, it will arouse
the interest of absorbed attention and
horror-stricken suspense.   It is the latter course that was followed by Joseph
Hatton in the construction of his melodrama of *John Needham's Double*, and a
practical and cogent motive to the effect
thus indicated, — which is a feeling compounded of eager curiosity, shocked and
startled perception, and feverish wonder
and excitement, — was the dramatic re-

sult that he obtained. *John Needham's Double* had its first representation upon any stage February 4, 1891, in Palmer's theatre, New York. It is ingenious in mechanism. It arouses and sustains a painful anxiety. It enthralls the spectator's attention. It is written in a nervous, fluent style, and it contains no particle either of the dulness of didacticism or the tediousness of literary vanity. A thread not precisely of humour, but of vivacious spirit, runs through it, and so it is not unduly saturated with the sombre colour that commonly invests the stage picture of crime.

Attention centres on the crime of murder. There are two men who bear to each other a resemblance so exact that not only casual acquaintances but even old friends and close relatives might mistake the one for the other. Norbury is a country squire, genial, comfortable, serene, living only to do good, and loved by all who know him. He is a widower, but his only sister resides with him, and is tenderly devoted to his welfare. Needham is a man of business, resident in London, an ambitious, unscrupulous man, to whom money is a god and who lives for power. Those men are super-

ficially alike, and chance brings them together at a moment of such supreme
significance in the fortunes of each that it
proves fatal to both. Norbury has just inherited a fortune in America, which he
must cross the ocean to obtain. Needham
has met with disasters, has resorted to
forgery in order to save his credit, is finan-
cially ruined, and now stands on the verge
of bankruptcy, exposure, and the penalty
for crime. At this crisis Norbury and
Needham meet, and out of their close resemblance to each other springs a momentary intimacy. Momentary though it be,
however, it is sufficient to seal the fate of
Norbury and to accomplish the damnation
of Needham. The one man is simple,
credulous, confiding; the other, specious,
concentrated, desperate, deadly. Norbury,
already separated from his home, and now
in London and about to embark for America, tells his story to Needham, and so puts
himself into the hands of the assassin. On
the night before the day appointed for his
sailing he is lured to Needham's home and
there he is murdered. In the morning his
body is found, and it is supposed to be that
of Needham, dead by his own hand. Needham, meanwhile, has become Norbury, and

in that character he assumes and accomplishes the dead man's mission. But Norbury's sister, who has seen the murder in a dream, will not be satisfied. She follows to America, to seek her brother; she confronts the impostor; and, although at first startled and perplexed as to the resemblance, she beats down his guard at last, by producing his mother to establish his identity; and thereupon — to escape that final test and not to break the heart of the mother whom, alone, out of all the world, the villain loves — he swallows poison and so expires.

The play consists of three acts. In act one you look upon the cheerful country home of Norbury, and upon the man himself, surrounded by friends and comforts. It is the time of roses and all the world seems consecrated to beauty. Into that picture comes the figure of John Needham, and from that moment there is a chill in the air. Early in the act the author has touched a note of omen, and, iterated by many subtle devices, that undertone of dark presentiment thenceforward goes sounding on, with its presage of impending peril that no one will heed. In the second act you see the foredoomed Norbury departing from his London hotel, on the last walk that he is ever to take; and a little later you see him welcomed by Needham in his lonely home, and suddenly and savagely put to death; and then you see Norbury, impersonated by his assassin, re-enter his hotel and resume his interrupted life. The scenes were of astonishing vitality and wonderfully fine effect — for there, as throughout the piece, Willard played both Norbury and Needham, changing from one to the other with great celerity, and, while maintaining the likeness, discriminating between the two individualities with a subtlety and precision that were marvellous. Once, at the moment before the murder, the two men are together upon the stage; but it is in a dimly lighted room and adroit use of a double had to be made for the consummation of the effect. Willard, of all the actors that have been seen, curiously blends the cynic with the saint. In *The Middleman* and *Judah* he presented characters prompted by goodness. As John Needham he presented a character of such baleful and sinister depravity as well might chill the blood — for, in its fidelity, its infernal wickedness, and its gaunt and grisly power, it conveyed suggestions of the possible evil in human nature that were almost too horrible for thought. Not often in a long experience of the acted drama has such an image been seen of implacable evil and stealthy and fatal doom as Willard presented when, in the character of Needham he was awaiting his victim in the dark and lonely house — from which all but himself have departed, and in which the sound of the sudden bell only serves to make the solitude more desolate and the danger more grim. A little later, and in violent and striking contrast with that scene of shuddering horror, you saw the same man, in his light, genial, specious mood of rosy benignity — under which all the while lurked an icy and devilish craft — getting point by point that investiture with another man's rights which was to make his duplicity victorious, and give him, in a new world, a new career, built on murder and theft. Would such a man weaken and surrender at the sound of his mother's voice? It seems unlikely, yet it is not impossible. Willard impersonated Needham in such a manner as to suggest a strain of weakness in his nature. It was a performance of extraordinary variety and force. The concentration with which it sustained intense mental excitement is a virtue only possible where there is a commanding brain, a puissant will, and a great reserve of repose.

The weakness of Needham shows itself at last in the unnerved tension of an apprehensive mind. Fine intelligence suffers, and suffers as much as tender sensibility. Such a man as Willard made John Needham to be would know his polluted state, in all its hideous depravity, and in all the horror of predestinate retribution. The gradual subsidence of vitality was indicated with excellent skill. As one peril succeeds to another, and his fatal secret is struggling to escape, the wretched man has recourse to brandy. It was the old story of human frailty vainly defiant of eternal law, established and operant in the human soul. The subtlety with which Willard perceived that, and the ease with which he expressed it, were superb. Treated in that way a melodramatic character is invested with the unusual dignity of tragical significance and moral admonition.

XXIII.

RISTORI.

ADELAIDE RISTORI made her first appearance in America at the theatre in Fourteenth street, New York, on September 20, 1866. Her first engagement, including her provincial tour, lasted eight months, ending on May 17, 1867. She gave, in that time, one hundred and sixty-eight performances. The parts that she acted were Medea, Mary Stuart, Queen Elizabeth, Phædre, Judith, Pia de Tolomei, Francesca da Rimini, Adrienne Lecouvreur, Tisbe, Camma, Myrrha, Deborah, Norma, and Lady Macbeth. Her second engagement in America began on September 18, 1867, and lasted nine months — ending on June 26, 1868. She gave, in that time, one hundred and eighty-one performances — fifty-six of them being given in the island of Cuba. The chief new parts that she then played were Marie Antoinette and Isabella Suarez. The drama of *Marie Antoinette* was acted for the first

time on October 7, 1867. Both engagements
were directed by Jacob Grau. In New York
she always played — save for an odd occasion now and then — at the Fourteenth-street
theatre, and the most important periods
in the history of that variable house are
those which are associated with her name.
Ristori's third and farewell engagement
began March 2, 1875, and she was seen as
Queen Elizabeth, Mary Stuart, Medea, Lu-
crezia Borgia, Marie Antoinette, Myrrha,
the heroine of *The Huguenots,* and in the
sleep-walking scene — in English — from
Macbeth.

The conquering characteristic of Ristori's
acting was its humanity. She was faithful
to actual life ; and that fidelity appeared in
her presentment of classic ideals as well as
in her portraiture of the heroines of history.
She was not a spiritual actress ; her art
methods were, distinctively, rugged rather
than delicate ; and her mind seemed deficient in the attribute of poetry. But all of
her dramatic persons were women of flesh
and blood, and she was always definite in
depicting them. She ranked in the school
of natural, as contrasted with the school of
ideal, tragedians. Those thinkers upon
acting who attach more value to imagination

in conceiving of ideals, and to intellectual
character in expressing them, than to frenzies of the person and the eccentricities of
ebullient emotion, were able, while rejoic-
ing in her magnetism, to enjoy it with something of the coolness of patience. She was,
unquestionably, a great actress; she possessed many attributes, physical and mental, which made her one of the foremost
women of her time; but she lacked the in-
effable quality which has always been found
to animate and hallow the highest forms of
human genius.

The moods and conditions of human nature and experience that Ristori best portrayed are — with little exception — those
that result from conflicts in the impassioned
heart and amidst the amorous physical passions. She could express, in absolute perfection, the fury of a woman scorned. Her
manifestations of ferocity, the wild anguish
of remorse, and the delirium of desolation
were tremendous, alike in their effect and
their depth. The roots of that art, however, did not strike into the ideal. The
springs of it arose in the earth. Ristori's
influence upon the stage was steadily ennobling, and she stored remembrance with
many splendid images. In her Mary Stu-

art the spectator saw religious exaltation
and tender pathos ; and that performance gave a distinct idea of her extraordinary reserve power. In Elizabeth her
utmost of achievement was conflict betwixt love and pride, closely succeeded by
a delirium of fury and an awful collapse
of remorse — showing the desolation of a
heart-broken woman and of a self-con-
demning queen, conscious of lost innocence
and of a fearful burden of sin. In Camma
she exhibited a terrible conflict of passions,
in a nature saturated with misery, hatred,
and the furious purpose of vengeance. Her
Myrrha was overwhelming as a portrayal
of the condition of insanity consequent
upon incestuous passion. The womanhood
was beautiful, the passion fierce, the death
ecstatic. Her Norma, like her Medea, was
chiefly victorious as a type of luxuriant animal vitality, exhibiting — under the shap-
ing pressure of experience — rage, scorn,
the tenderness of the female leopard, the
delirium of outraged love and wounded
pride, and the pathos of abject misery.
Her loveliest personations were Marie
Antoinette, Isabella Suarez, and Pia de
Tolomei. As Norrina, in the play of *I
Pazzi per Progetto*, she imparted a de-

licious impression of the sunny side of
her artistic nature. Comparing Ristori
with herself, her Lady Macbeth, Adrienne Lecouvreur, Deborah, and Tisbe
were representative and explanatory fail-
ures. Her Lady Macbeth was a murderous
Italian virago. Her Deborah was insipid.
Her Tisbe was over-mature and unspirit-
ual. Her Adrienne was artificial, and it
lacked both tenderness and the essential
element of inherent sadness; but it was
powerful — as all her works were, at certain points — and the comedy of it was
well compounded of archness and fire.
The spell of her individuality ceased to
command as soon as she left the sphere
of melodramatic tragedy; but within that
sphere she was peerless. In the realm of
the literal, the actual, she had no rival unless it were Salvini. In the imaginative,
the ideal, she has been surpassed: but the
epoch was not without cause for pride and
gratitude that could name Charlotte Cushman, Marie Seebach, and Adelaide Ristori
as contemporaries and as its own.

XXIV.

SARAH BERNHARDT'S ACTING.

THE character of Phædre was a great character as represented by Rachel, and each successor to that illustrious actress has seemed to recognise the necessity of emulating her renown in that classic tragedy. Phædre was in the repertory of Matilda Heron, and it has been acted by Ristori, Seebach, Janauschek, and Modjeska. The stage has long been acquainted with it but happily has seldom been compelled to endure it. Sarah Bernhardt played it because Rachel did, and because her towering ambition and restless spirit court every ordeal of difficulty. It cannot be said that she chose Phædre because the character is either suited to her nature, or fitted to display the attributes of her art — for she was not like it and she was not free in it.

The adequate representative of Phædre must have at least two attributes in abundance that Sarah Bernhardt has not shown;

majesty and tenderness. Taste recognises in Phædre a lofty ideal of majestic womanhood forced by fate to yield itself to a consuming passion ; to suffer agonies of self-contempt and remorse for that degrading, irresistible sin ; and at last to expiate its offence against itself, and against ideal purity, by self-destruction. The theme is horribly painful. In dramatic presentation it can only be redeemed by a temperament and a method of acting that place great emphasis on spiritual remorse and lift the personality far above actual life.

Sarah Bernhardt did not so redeem it, but applied to that character the passion of Camille with the method of Adrienne — the natural style, in other words, to a subject entirely unnatural, a piece designedly conceived and written in close imitation of the Greek form. "Impassive, stilted, and sententious" are the adjectives that Alexandre Dumas employed to describe the classic drama of France ; and they describe it well. This particular specimen of it is the last work that judicious taste would think of selecting for a natural, modern, familiar interpretation. Phædre should be the white-marble statue, veined with golden fire ; not the glittering Parisian belle.

Sarah Bernhardt accomplished all that could be done by a woman whose destiny it is — speaking of destiny as the consequence of character — to fascinate but not to be fascinated. The best of her art was the expression of terrible passion. Like Rachel she revealed the ravaged condition of Phædre's mind at the outset, and thus at once excited a feeling of pity, while deftly preparing the way for the awful, agonizing culmination of her deplorable experience. But she never attained to majesty ; she but dimly gave the idea of an impelling, inexorable fate ; and there was more love of self than of anybody else in her portraiture of what was intended to depict the operation of love. The most startling moment, perhaps, was that in which Phædre's frenzy precipitates the disclosure of her fatal secret to Hippolyte. The alternations of self-pitying lamentation with explosive protest were made with intense power, and the beauty of the elocution was superlative. Throughout her performance, indeed, the play of voice was fascinating with sweetness and impressive with eloquence. It could not be doubted that every phase of Phædre's horrible suffering was, at least, recognised through feminine intuition.

Sarah Bernhardt produced a thrilling effect with her maddened, despairing utterance of the accession of jealousy to the troubles already so massive and intolerable. The piece, however, affords few dramatic situations. The action is of the kind that passes within the breast — a strife of strong passions in conflict — and this induces copious soliloquy and conversation, much of which is tedious. Sarah Bernhardt was at times monotonous and lachrymose, in her recital of the rhymed anguish of the great Racine. Her strength — although it was reserved with skill — did not suffice to sustain her throughout the fearful struggle and the long-drawn vociferations that mainly compose the tragedy. The moments of her action that linger pleasantly in memory are those in which — lapsing into involuntary dreaminess — she murmured the sensuous delight of a fulfilled passion. At other fortunate points in the representation she impressed most deeply by the attitude and countenance of strained nervous concentration. Her appearance was a picture. She wore white robes, embroidered with gold, and no colour, and she looked the personification of wasting misery. The performance defined and deepened the impression that

Sarah Bernhardt is a strong actress only in parts that are built upon the senses and the morbid emotions — not upon the heart. The morbid part of Phædre was conveyed as fully and as truly as could be wished; but the heart was left out of the ideal, and the tone of the mechanism was lowered by over "natural" treatment. It is significant that this actress has never succeeded in portraying either a great woman or a lovely woman. Her embodiment of Phædre was a comparative failure, from its lack of majesty, tenderness, and spiritual remorse; and the chief charm of her embodiment of Dona Sol was the half sensuous, half poetic glamour with which she invested an amorous ecstasy. The dramatic individualities in which she has appeared to be most potential and most brilliant are those viciously erratic or openly wicked individualities in which, nevertheless, there are qualities of animal sensibility. Her most characteristic embodiments — unique, massive, splendid, and strong in their integrity and affluence of evil — were Fedora and Theodora. Seeing Sarah Bernhardt in those two characters you see absolutely all that her nature has the mission or the power to disclose. She might present one aspect of

Shakespeare's Cleopatra, but such women as Shakespeare's Constance and Hermione she could not embody, and probably could not understand. In whatever character she might undertake, her dramatic art would be delicate in texture and felicitous in method. The thing done by her was often repulsive ; the manner of doing it was often superb. A dramatic artist of the highest order is one who is capable of communicating to other souls the ennobling benefits of beauty. A dramatic artist of the next rank is one who conquers by personal singularity combined with professional expertness.

The drama of *Theodora* is the image of a carnal intrigue conducted by the wife of the Emperor Justinian, which is attended by incidents of strife, peril, and murder, which culminates in detection, and terminates in a violent and hideous death. It would be difficult to imagine a character that combines attributes of a more hateful description than those which are blended in *Theodora*. The essential fibres of that person are vanity and selfishness. Around those are crystallised craft, sensuality, duplicity, cruelty, haughty insolence and flippant recklessness. That compound, incarnated in a supple and beautiful physique, is redeemed by fierce courage, indomitable determination, a resolute will, and signal capacity for the administration of public affairs. The point upon which the dramatist more particularly relies for the artistic redemption of that wicked woman is her capacity for sincerity in a sexual attachment. Once, at least, she loves, in her tiger-like fashion, and — as if that were at all extraordinary or in the least palliative of moral deformity — the observer is, apparently, expected to admire her on that account. Sarah Bernhardt is accredited with having expressed the opinion that *Theodora* is "grand" and "beautiful," — affording great opportunities for the actor and for stage effect. That is more or less a question of taste. There really is something higher and finer in this life than the sexual love of a wanton stage-heroine and the perturbation attendant upon her career of vice and crime. It is true, however, that, after a languid and prolix opening, the play begins to present situations which are both pictorial and dramatic. No one but a devotee of the personality of Bernhardt could fail to be bored by the first two acts, and no one but an actress profoundly saturated with self-complacency could linger upon their trivial

details with anything like Sarah Bernhardt's
deliberation. The couch business, the reception of Belisarius, the visit to the menagerie, the quest of the love-philter, the
fooling with the wild beasts — all was slow
and dull; but at many points in the course of
the later acts Sarah Bernhardt loosed her
fiery impetuosity, making successive situations of passion and of peril luminous and
eloquent. No one could better express than
she did the mood and the magic of Delilah,
in the scene of her lover's subjugation. The
defiance of the emperor was an electrical
moment. The celerity of her despatch of
the captured accomplice, whom she stabs to
the heart with a bodkin caught suddenly
out of her hair, was superb in its dramatic
fitness. Few stage visions have been seen
of such imperial magnificence as she incarnated in *Theodora's* procession to the
throne, and her assumption of royal state
beside her consort. It cannot be said too
strongly that the essential illusion of the
drama was created and sustained by Sarah
Bernhardt not less through identification
with the character than by artistic skill and
the expert appliance of ingenious accessories. She got inside of the character and
lived in it, and she made you feel that this

was true : but, when all is said, you had only
seen a beautiful devil. To what extent that
does you any good, to what extent it is
worth while, you must determine for yourself. Fashions are mutable. It is not the
delirium or the eccentricity that refreshes
or endures.

Sarah Bernhardt has not at any time
exhibited such tragic power as she displayed
in bringing the emotion of the empress to
the climax of the fatal catastrophe. The
menagerie scene was not marred by the in-
troduction of actual beasts. The raiment
worn by Bernhardt, as Theodora, was
opulent and gorgeous ; but the expres-
sive suitability of the dresses, — as denoted
for instance, by the snake-sleeves worn in
the circus, — was more remarkable and
more praiseworthy than their costly beauty.

With reference to all persons who appear upon the stage it may be surmised
that they are well contented with themselves ; for if they were not they would
shrink from the public attention instead of
seeking it. That complacency, no doubt,
is an amiable weakness. Nobody com-
plains of it. The public, which often is
pleased and sometimes is benefited by the
ministrations of actors, has no reason to

object to it.   Yet that complacency, which
has its pleasant side, has also its comic side
and its painful side.   The latter aspects
of it were illustrated in the professional
proceedings of Sarah Bernhardt, whose
emergence in the character of Sardou's
Cleopatra again claimed for herself the
admiring attention of the public, and again
sought to substantiate that claim by presenting yet another type of egregious vanity
and morbid folly.   In Cleopatra, precisely
as in La Tosca, the accomplished French
actress displayed herself, her faculties, and
her peculiarities with liberal prodigality,
and with abundant and often admirable
technical skill.   But the chief impression
that she conveyed, and the essential drift of
thought that she stimulated, were philosophic rather than professional.   There
may be persons to whom the stage embodiment of a licentious and ferocious female is
impressive and delightful — a thing worthy
to be achieved and desirable to be seen.
It was noticed by the philosopher Locke
that the world has people of all sorts.   But
for a sane and thoughtful observer the impression left by Sarah Bernhardt's performance of Cleopatra was an impression of
regret that a woman so clever should make

herself so trivial, and that an actress of so
much talent should not be able to find a
better use for her powers than the paltry
and ignominious employment of presenting
an ideal of womanhood that degrades it to
the level of the tiger and the ape. For this
discrepancy there can be but one cause.
The statement of it goes to the root of the
subject of Sarah Bernhardt's acting. The
mental constitution of that actress is devoid
of greatness, and, while her temperament
is dramatic and her executive faculties are
extraordinary, the animating spirit, the
individuality, is frivolous. The line upon
which she walks is the line to which nature
has restricted her.

No impulse other than that of colossal
vanity would prompt, or would permit, any
woman to come into the public view in such
a character as that of Sardou's Cleopatra.
The part has not one fibre of nobility to
exalt it, or one touch of poetry to beautify
it, or one thrill of heroism to redeem it.
In the character of Cleopatra which has
commonly been known upon the English
stage, — the character as drawn by Shakespeare, — there is a tremendous animal
appetite ; but also there are splendid qualities of heart, mind, and imagination

mingled with it. That great poet did not
seek to concentrate attention simply upon
an erotic fool. He magnified his historic
original and invested it with a glory that in
actual life it never possessed. Sardou's
Cleopatra, on the contrary, is the futile
incarnation of vain, voluptuous wantonness
— the sleek, supple sensuality of the cat,
together with its crafty vigilance, its selfish
caprice, its treacherous spite, and its pitiless ferocity. Seeing that personage you
see womanhood at its worst. On every
side of the picture the limit is the carnal
limit. No great word is spoken. No great
action is performed. No high impulse is
indicated. No sweet or fine feeling is
entertained in the piece or awakened in
the auditor. Effrontery and depravity,
sprinkled over with gewgaws, make up the
sum of the matter. An unchaste and un-
principled woman, successful by means of
her physical fascination, is depicted as
triumphant over an infatuated man, old
enough to be wise, but not strong enough
to act according to his knowledge. That is
the substance of the drama. The bog of
sensuality is opened before you, and upon
that you are desired to gaze and moralise.
You behold a Parisian tableau of Samson

and Delilah, decked out in Roman and
Egyptian garments, and you watch the
process of subjugation of a man by a
woman. Man and woman are alike ordinary. There is nothing splendid about
them except their furniture and their raiment. There is nothing great about them
except their conceit. At first they are at
a feast, and presently they agree to part for
awhile, and then Cleopatra, who has become physically enamoured of her burly
captive, is seen to be longing for him and
to trample on a bearer of the ill-news of his
marriage. A little later, you observe her
jealous fury when she sees her errant lover
in the companionship of another woman,
and you listen to her insane invocation that
a tempest may burst forth and waste the
universe. Presently she is again in possession of her plaything; and then she ruins
him as a soldier in order to show her power
over him as an animal. Last of all, you
see her application of an actual reptile to
her person — and the silly spectacle is
ended. All this while your mind has never
once been liberated from the confines of a
dismal treatise on the low instincts of
human nature and the mean aspects of
human conduct. You have seen an expe-

rienced actress represent, with absolute
fidelity, a modern French coquette, be-
dizened to look like something that is
supposed to be Egyptian; but neither in
the historic nor in the dramatic point
of view has anything been gained. You
are neither correctly informed, nor nobly
agitated, nor finely impressed. The story
of Antony and Cleopatra, as it is told in
Sardou's piece, is not the authentic account of them that may be read in Plutarch, but a garbled version of it. The
only effective dramatic passage in the play
is one that, obviously, was suggested by a
familiar and better passage in Shakespeare
— the scene which, probably, Shakespeare
based on Plutarch's narrative of Cleopatra's
assault on Seleucus. And, finally, Antony
and Cleopatra — characters that Shakespeare's glorious imagination and splendid
treatment have sublimated and half redeemed — are made, by the French author,
to be trivial, vapid, and base; a pair of
modern story-paper lovers, solicitous for
nothing but their conjunctive loves, and, to
any person having a proper comprehension
of the dignity of human life, a vulgar and
wearisome impertinence.

It is not material that Sarah Bernhardt

dressed the wanton, expeditious, and tumultuous Cleopatra in gorgeous raiment
and embodied her with theatrical skill.
She is an old and experienced actress, and
it would be strange, indeed, if she were not
able to present in an effective manner a
part so simple as that of the posturing,
picture-making heroine of a spectacle-
drama. Effective although it was, however,
her performance of Cleopatra, in one aspect
of it, could not escape being comical. A
woman must be exceedingly beautiful, and
— more than beautiful — she must be poeti-
cally enchanting, if she would cause such
a character as Sardou's Cleopatra to be
accepted seriously. Such a woman, in appearance, as Louisa Nisbett must have been,
might, perhaps, have made that part potential, by the luminous and intoxicating
charm of personal loveliness. Sarah Bernhardt, although a woman of striking physi-
ognomy, great nervous vitality, insinuating
ways, and, above all, a wonderfully clear,
flexible, melodious, penetrating, and ex-
pressive voice, cannot be said distinctively
to possess beauty or the quality of enchantment. Formidable and aggressive natures
may command, and that way they may
prevail ; but they do not entice. During

the whole of Sarah Bernhardt's almost
interminable performance of Cleopatra
there was not one instant when any rational observer could forget that she was
working the wires of professional machinery. Those wires were worked exceedingly
well by her, for she was always graceful
and generally adroit; but, except to the
eyes of inexperience, or of mistaken enthusiasm, or of servile idolatry, they created
no illusion; and as you contemplated the
well-managed, seductive blandishments and
sinuous gyrations, the concentrated furies
and the explosive ebullitions, of the expert
and facile performer the idea was never
far from your amused thought of a middle-
aged lady, blessed with a grown-up family,
who is roaming up and down the world
to smirk, to bridle, to purr, to posture, to
curvet, and to tantalise, and thus to show
to theatrical audiences the regulation behaviour of a cyprian when she wishes to
turn a man into a fool. The proficient
actress was, of course, evident. No one
would think of denying or disparaging
Sarah Bernhardt's dramatic ability and
ample and various dramatic equipment.
She was not nearly as impressive in Cleopatra, however, as she was in La Tosca —

one reason, perhaps, being that the former play is not as strong as the latter. The most of Sardou's *Cleopatra* is pageantry. When the piece was shown in Paris local newspapers said that it was "a play for exportation"; and they could not well have expressed their contempt for it in more significant words. The pervading technical defect of Sarah Bernhardt's acting in it flowed from obvious artifice. That defect was metallic insincerity of feeling blended with saccharine monotony of expression.

The time has been when people who went to the theatre went there with the rational expectation that they were to see something refined, intellectual, and noble; that they were to be pleased, cheered, charmed, impressed, elevated above the commonplace, ennobled and benefited, and in that way made better and happier. The appeal then made by the theatre was an appeal to the better feelings and the finer faculties of the human mind, and it was made with taste, scholarship, and refinement. The votary of the stage could follow it without loss of self-respect and could see and remember a play without mortification and disgust. The mental associations that were formed with actors were fruitful of

fine fancies, gentle thoughts, and lovely
ideals.   All this is, in some degree,
changed; and nothing in the present theatrical time more distinctly marks this
change than the acceptance and therefore
practical success of such a narrow, fantastic, morbid, artistic eccentricity as Sarah
Bernhardt has continually shown herself to
be — an actress who habitually appears in
dramas that are mostly nightmares, and
who scarcely ever presents, or even tries
to present, a type of womanhood that can
be seen without shame or remembered
without abhorrence.   There need not be
hesitation in speaking plainly of such a
matter. It is not the annalist of the passing
stage who obtrudes upon public attention
the Fedoras and Theodoras and Toscas
and Cleopatras, the diseased deformities
of a lawless fancy, a perverse ingenuity,
and a sickly mind ; it is the public performer who introduces those things to the
public knowledge, and who compels the
consideration of them — that public performer who has chosen to embellish and
illustrate her professional progress with
skeletons, and coffins, and monkeys, and
tiger-cats, and snakes, till at length her
name, which ought to be that of a renowned

actress, and which, as such, it would be a
delight to honour, has become the absolute
synonym of dramatic extravagance, affectation, and folly.

The assertion that the person and the
artist are entirely distinct, and that they
must never be viewed as one, is a part of
the critical cant of the day, and it may
always be expected to arise as a shield for
every offence against those artistic laws of
beauty which ought to govern and protect
the stage. A work of art should be contemplated as a work of art, and as nothing
else. But the artist — in whatsoever line
of art he may operate — who expects to
create an artistic work without putting his
soul into it, and without disclosing his
moral and spiritual as well as his intellectual nature, is ignorant of even the first
elements and simplest laws of life. The
acting is the actor. Through the one you
see the other — for it steadily shines upon
you and could not conceal itself if it would.
You may, if you like, ostensibly ignore it
in the discussion of the particular artistic
achievement ; but the man is always behind
the work, and you will find, upon analysis,
that your views of anything that has been
made invariably depend upon your percep-

tion of the being that made it.   The acting
of Sarah Bernhardt cannot be separated
from her personality.   The moment she
tries to depart from herself she fails — as
she conspicuously did in the classic Phædre, and as she inevitably would in such a
part as the woman-like Imogen or the di-
vinely majestic Queen Katherine of Shakespeare.   This may be a reason why the
distinguished French actress adheres to her
chosen course : it is not a reason why her
professional proceedings should be admired
and extolled by those who think, and who
are conscious of an intellectual and moral
responsibility to the public in what they
say.

XXV.

COQUELIN AS TARTUFFE.

THE excellence of Molière's comedy of
Tartuffe consists in its contrasts of
character, its pictorial fidelity to life, its
felicities of dialogue, and its scathing rebuke
of sanctimonious hypocrisy. Tartuffe is that
meanest and most loathsome of impostors,
the licentious scoundrel who conceals a de-
praved heart and a life of sensual indul-
gence beneath the mask of religious zeal
and moral self-abnegation. Many varia-
tions of that type of man — such, for example, as Maworm, Dr. Cantwell, Aminidab
Sleek, and Joseph Surface — have been displayed, during many years, upon the English-speaking stage. The most elaborately
drawn and most brilliant hypocrite of all is
Joseph Surface — just as *The School for
Scandal* is the most powerful, sparkling,
and trenchant play, upon the subject of
moral imposture, that has been written, not
excepting Ben Jonson's *Volpone*.

Molière's comedy is somewhat deficient in

interest of plot and in the element of action. The first two acts are devoted to a description of circumstances, the posing of the characters, and the work of preparation. Tartuffe does not enter till act third. In that act he makes a licentious proposal to the wife of the friend in whose home he has established himself, and being repulsed and in danger of exposure, contrives to blind that friend still further by an adroit assumption of fault, repentance, and humility. In act fourth he is exposed by the wife, who leads him to avow his base passion, in the hearing of her husband, concealed under a table. Then he assumes his real character, that of a cruel and relentless villain, and he is only prevented from ruining the friend who has clothed and fed him by the intervention of royal authority. There are two effective scenes in the piece, which culminates with the exposure of Tartuffe — development of character, and not of plot, being the purpose of the comedy.

Tartuffe may be acted in at least two ways. The author appears to have conceived him as a plump, florid, sleek individual, with a fluent delivery and with a bland and specious demeanour of affected meek-

ness.   Such persons are, in actual life, usually made known to close observers by the
eye, which is hard and bold in expression,
fat and watery, crafty when aware of being
observed, and horribly carnal and cruel
when under the influence of stimulant.   An
assumption of oily good humour is not unusual with that type of villain, but he is
more commonly grave, polished, and insid-
ious.   The latter image of him is the one
usually presented on the stage, and probably it is the one that Molière intended —
because the one that is the most dramatic.
M. Coquelin presented a suave, easy-going,
knavish rascal, self-indulgent and genial,
except at certain moments of peril and of
defensive pugnacity.   His vein was more
that of Aminidab Sleek than that of Joseph
Surface.   Simple animal appetite, rather
than calculating sentimental luxurious sensuality, was asserted as a predominant motive, and the effect of hateful wickedness
was thus subordinated to that of physical
bulk and a curiously humorous inertia.   It
is hardly conceivable that Burton, with his
fine intellect, would have acted Tartuffe
upon that theory ; but if he had so acted it,
he would have been latently comical in M.
Coquelin's manner — only he would have

been more comical. That hint may serve
to clarify description of M. Coquelin's art.
A subtle drollery seemed just beneath the
surface, and where that was absent the
colouring was dull. M. Coquelin assumed
gravity, but it was heavy rather than imposing. The affectation of contrition, at
the end of act third, was indeed a fine
stroke of nature, made with exquisite art.
There was excitement, but not an attractive
or plausible amatory ardour in Tartuffe's
declaration to the wife ; there was only an
exultant sense of desire and of the good fortune of possessing a priestly robe convenient
for the concealment of sin. More than
once, indeed, the rogue seemed to be laughing at himself, and taking his depravity, and
the trouble occasioned by him, as a joke.
The embodiment was framed, fashioned,
and illumined with fine intelligence and
ripe and assured mimetic skill ; but surely
there is more in Tartuffe than swinish ani-
malism. The personation of it ought to
shock with rapacious lust, hateful malice,
and a subtle, grisly spirit of crafty, wicked
intellect, as well as to amuse by surface
traits of humorous hypocrisy and comic
cynicism. The justification for the revival
of such a play as *Tartuffe* is that its hide-

ous central figure should be so truthfully
and well presented as to be made loathsome
and hateful. It is not so important that the
audience should be amused with an almost
droll impostor as that it should be made to
detest a vile and impious wretch. M. Coquelin's artistic method of making sport was
often superb — as when the priest told the
lady not to trouble about "Heaven." A
man may display great talent in acting,
even when he does the dubious thing; but
to do the precisely right thing and do it
superbly is the best success. The personation of Tartuffe was one of M. Coquelin's
most intellectual achievements, and it explained his peculiar fame.

Behind the question of technical proficiency in the art of acting there is always
the question of individual superiority and
of what may be called artistic beneficence
— the question, in other words, whether
the actor has been supremely endowed by
nature, and is therefore of extraordinary
worth and importance to the community.
M. Coquelin does not exercise the puissant and predominant magic of genius.
He does not fascinate either by inherent,
spontaneous charm, or by the loveliness of
acquired grace. He is deficient of personal

distinction. In the atmosphere of poetry, romance and passion — as was conspicuously shown by his Don Cæsar — he is out of place. He is not an imaginative actor. On the other hand, M. Coquelin is possessed of a subtle perception of character, and he is a consummate master of the art of portraying it — only, since his temperament is cold, he cannot always simulate the excitement that is essential to make acting seem natural by a perfect concealment of art. He has strength of character, force of brain, signified in mental poise and will, and an affluent fund of droll humour. His self-possession is extraordinary, showing itself in the repose and deliberate precision with which he elaborated every portion of every character. His best achievements were those of the low comedian, — the artistic delineator of Dogberry, Roderigo, Pistol, Moses, Acres, and Tony Lumpkin, which are low-comedy parts, although it is possible to act some of them with a high-comedy touch. M. Coquelin's tendencies are toward the broadly comic aspects of human personality, the grotesque attributes of character, the mirth and absurdity of men and of experience. And he has depicted those aspects of nature with admirable fidelity.

XXVI.

HELENA MODJESKA.

HELENA MODJESKA was born at Cracow, in Poland, in 1844. Her maiden name was Helen Benda. At the age of seventeen she was married to a gentleman named Modezejewska, with whom she lived till his death, in 1865. That name she shortened, for stage use, into Modjeska. Her first appearance on the stage was made in 1862 at Bochnia, and she has been an actress ever since. In 1868 she became the wife of Count Charles Bozenta Chlapowski, a patriot who had been concerned in the Polish insurrection of 1863. After her marriage she entered upon the Warsaw stage, and made a brilliant hit as Adrienne Lecouvreur ; but she soon returned to Cracow, where the Count Chlapowski was managing a political journal, and where she plunged into politics. Later she went back to the Warsaw theatre — the Count Chlapowski having determined to resign his editorial responsibilities and devote his en-

ergies to her advancement as an actress.
At Warsaw Modjeska acted many parts,
and she aroused much jealousy and envy,
both in social circles and on the stage,
so that the Polish capital became almost
uninhabitable. That fact, together with
domestic afflictions, led the Count and
Countess Chlapowski to emigrate, and in
1876 they arrived in California, where for
a short time they lived on a farm, and
where Modjeska learned English. In 1877
the actress appeared at the California theatre in San Francisco, and on December 22
in that year she was first seen in New York,
at the Fifth-avenue theatre. Her career
since then has been in the beaten track
of routine and prosperity. She revisited
Poland in 1879 and acted in several cities;
and in May 1880 she appeared at the
Court theatre, London, and afterward at
the Princess's, with much success. In
December 1881 she reappeared in America, and since that time she has steadily
pursued her vocation upon the American
stage. Her repertory, while she was at the
Imperial theatre in Warsaw, included more
than a hundred characters — among them
being Shakespeare's Juliet, Beatrice, Ophelia, Desdemona, Cordelia, Katherine, Queen

Anne, and Cleopatra; Goethe's Margaret, and also Phædre, Tisbe, Mary Stuart, and Joan of Arc. Upon the American stage she has embodied most of those parts, together with Adrienne Lecouvreur, Camille, Frou-Frou, Rosalind, Viola, Imogen, Queen Katherine, and Lady Macbeth — the last of these in association with Edwin Booth.

No artist more delicate and subtle than Modjeska has appeared among the women of the stage. Her power is limited, and she speaks the English language with a foreign cadence; but she has shown a rare dramatic intelligence, the atmosphere of her mind and art is poetic, and her execution is marked by exquisite refinement and grace. The works of an actress thus qualified must always impart pleasure, since she will set beautiful ideals clearly before the mind, give melodious utterance to poetic thoughts, express with sweetness the delicious traits of woman-like character, and exemplify with trained and competent skill the felicities of the dramatic art. Those persons who think that inspiration in acting is voluntary are likely sometimes to be disappointed in her, finding her cold. But Modjeska, like all true artists, has her great moments. The embodiment of Adrienne and Camille defined her genius and established her rank. The performance of Adrienne was not only beautiful in itself but massive and splendid in its denotements of the mind and soul behind it. It was an embodiment instinct with sensibility and with spiritual exaltation. It was the image of a woman who typifies exquisite natural refinement, consummate elegance of manners, and the sanctity and magnanimity of passionate love. It was more than the faithful and finished copy of a dramatic ideal: it was a revelation of the royal wealth of soul and supremacy of mind that make human nature sublime. To express the highest passion of which humanity is capable, and to express it as tempered by purity and nobility, is to accomplish the utmost that genius can reach. There are other and different peaks; but there is no higher one than that. Remembrance, dwelling on the method by which the actress sustained herself at that height, recalls that her intonation, gesture, movement, and play of countenance were spontaneous; that even her garments, devised and fashioned with sumptuous and delicate taste, seemed a part of the fibre and fragrance of the character; and that all her looks and actions sprang from and crystallised around her condition. The spectator could not know that she was acting, and art can do no more than to perfect and sustain the illusion that genius creates. This method, had it been absent, would have been missed, but present it was not noted. The looks of love — irradiated with happiness and irresistible in fascination — with which Adrienne's eyes were made to follow the form of her lover linger in memory as among the most beautiful and fortunate expedients of art; but it was the soul behind them which gave them power. Not since the days of Marie Seebach has any actress shown, as it was shown by Modjeska, in that performance, the union of emotional power — aroused through the imagination and not the senses — with intellectual character.

Modjeska did not bewilder with the ripe luxuriance of youthful beauty; her speech was slightly constrained by the fetters of a foreign language, and she painted life with the camel's-hair brush; but she diffused the fire of inspiration, the power of intensity — always as much more terrible than the power of violence as the silent lightning is more terrible than the crashing thunder — and she imparted that devastating thrill of passion which, to the big and blaring animals of the human race, is unknown. Love, as depicted by her, was the divine passion that exalts the heart and hallows the object by which it is evoked. Acting Adrienne Lecouvreur she had simply to give form and voice to an experience of that passion. Divested of all the intricacy of the plot — the dark-rooms, cross-purposes, back-stairways, kitchen-gardens, fatal snuff-boxes, tittle-tattle, and intrigue — Adrienne was depicted as a great woman who greatly loves; who is frenzied with bitter jealousy; who takes an imperial vengeance on her rival; who, thinking herself abandoned, falls into the hell of misery; whose magnanimous soul raises her above her fate; and who dies at last, the victim of hatred and cruelty, just as the clouds are lifting from her life. That experience Modjeska embodied in perfection. Not physically robust, she did not use in her art either the wind-mill or the flail. At the first view she attracted, but did not astonish, by elegance and harmony. It was only when — in the sequence of action — incident begins to affect feeling, and feeling to act upon character, that her powers unfolded

themselves and sprang to their victory. She
lived in the character. Her voice was sympathetic, and, in the low tones, very sweet.
Her face, in repose, — and afterward in the
lull of despair which, with a beautiful instinct of truth, she once introduced amid
her delirium, — was marked by feminine
sweetness and tender patience. Her move-
ments, always graceful, were sometimes
electrical in their rapidity and their long
and sinuous reach. Her innate grace —
shown in many ways, and notably in
Adrienne's delicate, high-bred recoil from
her lover's proffered kiss, so deft as scarcely
to be seen — was as sweet as the vanished
roses of some remembered June. In sorrow, in frenzy, and in the simulated agonies
of the death by poison, she never lapsed
out of the refinement of a gentlewoman.
Her performance of Adrienne satisfied that
craving for completeness in artistic effort
which is an instinct of the human mind,
and it taught how to suffer, how to endure,
and how, through the trial of sorrow, to rise
toward heaven.

Modjeska's embodiment of Camille (Mar-
guerite Gauthier), was not only beautiful
in spirit but supreme as a type of apparently spontaneous expression. Every-

thing was done that it is natural for Camille to do; and nothing was done that was not absolutely and essentially in her character. The poise of the personality was never dropped. Whether with a delicate, wayward wafture of the hand, or a little snap of the thumb and finger, or the flick of a lace handkerchief upon the little book of well-preserved accounts, the artist kept rigidly within her identity, and drew it and tinted it to the very hair-line of truth. The acting almost redeemed the subject. To feel a love which ought not to be felt and to accept a love which ought not to be accepted, is — always and inevitably — to prepare the way for bitter misery and undying anguish. From that result — from remorse, from self-torture, from pain that nothing can cure, and that all the success and pleasure upon earth can only for a while even alleviate — there is no escape. That lesson, and not another, was taught by Modjeska's Camille. There was in the representation an infinite pathos of dumb despair. The misery was such as a fallen angel might feel; the utterance of it such as only the gentlest of women and the most consummate of dramatic artists could achieve. Modjeska was best in the

interview with the father, who represents
fate, and the parting with the son, who
represents love and happiness. She was
the absolute image of magnificent wretchedness, and then of delirious anguish, in
the ball-room encounter; and she supplied,
in the beatific death scene, those elements of
pity, consolation, and religious faith which
alone can make the acted sacrifice justifiable. The expiation was felt to be then
complete; and from that death-bed the
awed thought arose into a trembling hope
of heaven — into the sacred feeling that sin
may at last be washed away, and the soul
that earth has stained be made white with
the Divine pardon. If anything could rec-
oncile judgment to the drama of *Camille* —
a piece that befogs moral perception and
perplexes all sentiments of right and duty
— it would be the embodiment of its heroine
by Modjeska. She was more like a spirit
than a woman; she was the ideal of native
purity, lost through passion, but struggling
toward the light of infinite mercy.

XXVII.

WILSON BARRETT AS YOUNG HAMLET.

THE first line spoken by Hamlet is, "A little more than kin and less than kind." That usually has been understood to mean, "I am a little more than a kinsman to you, because you, my uncle, have become my mother's husband; but I am a different sort of man." The line is a shaft of covert sarcasm. The shaft, however, is not hurled, because the words are spoken under the breath and are not intended to be heard. Wilson Barrett, in speaking that line, made the vowel short, in the word "kind," and sounded that word as if it were a rhyme for "sinned." The word "kind" he declares, is an old-country word for "child," and Hamlet's meaning is, "I am more than a kinsman to you, but less than a son." That makes the remark a mere statement of bald fact — such a statement as Hamlet, in his mood of bitter grief and resentment, would be but little likely to utter. There are times when the sorrow-stricken prince is forlorn and gentle; there never is a time when he is commonplace. Still, it may be assumed that Hamlet's bitterness of feeling underlies his words, whichever way you take them; and Wilson Barrett's textual emendation may, possibly, be correct. The point has no bearing upon the question of ideal.

When Hamlet comes upon the platform, in the first of his ghost scenes, the time being the middle of the night, and the night being apparently in late autumn, in the harsh climate of Denmark, he remarks that "the air bites shrewdly," and that "it is very cold." Wilson Barrett, speaking those words, turns the last half of the line into a question. "Is it very cold?" he asks; as if the Prince, already chilled, and therefore aware of the frigid temperature, were inquiring into the state of the royal thermometer. There are other details of verbal modification in Wilson Barrett's reading of the part, but they all show a striving after novelty, and they are insignificant. When Barry Sullivan's Hamlet rose to the surface, about 1858, that Hibernian Dane was heard to remark that he knew "a hawk from a hern. Pshaw!" This is about all that anybody now remembers of Mr. Sul-

livan's performance. It was not by his
"aitches" that John Philip Kemble became the Hamlet of his time. It is not by
verbal quirks that any actor ever rose, or
ever will rise, to the awful altitude of that
sublime conception.

Shakespeare begins the third act of
Hamlet with a "Room in the Castle," and
presently he changes the scene to a "Hall
in the same." In that Hall the play is
acted, which Hamlet has ordered the Players to represent before him, and to the
prospect of which he has entreated the
king and queen. That play-scene Wilson
Barrett presented in a garden. The idea,
probably, was derived from a hint in *Coxe's
Travels*, which mentions "Hamlet's Garden," adjacent to the Palace of Kronberg,
near Elsinore, in which tradition says that
the murder of the king was committed.
The actor thought that he could derive a
fine dramatic effect from causing Claudius
to behold the copy of his monstrous crime,
upon the actual spot — "within mine or-
chard" — where it was perpetrated. Upon
being told (he says) that the climate of
Northern Europe is cold, even on a night
in summer, for outdoor theatricals, he re-
plied that in the time of Hamlet open-air

theatres were customary. That position illustrates the fragile texture of his theory. There can be no serious objection to the use of a garden. Whatever will augment the legitimate dramatic effect of a play, without offence to reason, may rightly be introduced — for unless a play be effective it is useless. But, let the reason be plainly avowed. No theatres of any kind were in existence in Denmark in the time of Hamlet. Besides, if reference to the time of the play (the eleventh century) is to govern in one particular, why not in all? If we are to have Hamlet mounted and dressed according to local custom in the historic period of Fengon and Horvendile, most of the people in it must present themselves in skins — chiefly their own. And what authority would remain for Wilson Barrett's elaborate fencing play, in the scene of Hamlet's combat with Laertes? The art of foining, or defensive sword-play with the rapier and foil, did not come into fashion as a courtly practice until about the thirteenth century.

It is a worthy ambition that endeavours, in the stage-setting of a Shakespearian play, to harmonise the work in all its parts and to remove whatever disparities may have been left in it by the author. But that result is not always attainable. In general it can only be approximately reached. Every one of Shakespeare's plays that is acted has to be more or less cut. Almost every one of them is too long for representation, if left in its original state. *Hamlet*, in particular, has to be much condensed. Edwin Booth's version of it is the longest in use on the English-speaking stage, and Edwin Booth's version omits nearly one thousand lines of the original. The modern stage accomplishes much by picture that the old writers could only accomplish by language. Wilson Barrett's restorations, most of which are made subsequent to the closet scene, while they cast no new light upon the subject, had the effect of retarding the action — and of retarding it exactly at a point where the need of greater celerity has always been felt. Wilson Barrett, however, is an expeditious actor, and his Hamlet, whatever else may be true of it, was one of celerity.

The evidence derived from the text of *Hamlet* as printed in the *Folio* of 1623 specifically indicates Hamlet's age. He is thirty. The proof of that is found — as everybody knows — in the dialogue be-

tween Hamlet and the sexton. Wilson
Barrett's method of dispersing that evidence is radical. He declares that it does
not exist; that the text has been garbled;
that the original language of Shakespeare
has been altered; that expressions have
been introduced into that conversation between Hamlet and the clown which were not
written by Shakespeare but which were invented in order to make the language con-
formable to the requirements of various
old actors. He maintains that Hamlet
should be presented and accepted as a youth
of about eighteen; that Shakespeare has
drawn and described him as " young Hamlet," and that thirty is not "young." He
has adopted a theory, and he would therefore exclude from the tragedy whatever
language may happen to conflict with it.
That is a convenient method, but its valid-
ity is not recognised by Shakespeare
scholars. The words of the sexton — who
says that he has been a grave-digger since
" the very day that young Hamlet was
born," and that he has followed his " business," " man and boy, thirty years " — are
not, indeed, to be taken too literally.
" Man and boy," for instance, seems to be
no more than a loose phrase of common

parlance, used by a quaint Hodge whose
general style of thinking and of speech,
together with the senility of his fag-ends of
mis-remembered song, betoken an elderly
man — such a man as, in such an occupation, would be antique at fifty ; such a man
as would be noted rather for sly conceit
and dry and waggish humour than for
strict accuracy of reminiscence and nar-
ration. Still the text of the *Folio* of 1623
is a good basis of the authentic text of
Shakespeare. Its editors, Heminge and
Condell, affirm it printed from "his papers," — declaring that they "have scarce
received from him a blot" in them, — and
therefore a sensible reliance should be
placed on it. Obvious blunders in it ought
to be corrected ; and in good modern edi-
tions they mostly are corrected ; while
reference to the Second Quarto (the First,
which is understood to be this actor's
stronghold, being accounted piratical and
untrustworthy), sometimes procures clearer
and more felicitous readings. But arbi-
trary alterations, made without warrant or
proof, as restorations of Shakespeare's
original words or meanings, are not likely
to prosper. Wilson Barrett, following a
dubious conjecture, based on an old poem,

believes that a line in the fencing-scene,
"Our son is fat and scant of breath," is
spurious ; that it was foisted into the text
in order to suit the need of Richard Burbage, the first actor of Hamlet ; and he
reasons that if one line was inserted to
suit Burbage other lines may have been
inserted to suit other actors, and accordingly that you are justified in rejecting any
part of the text that you fancy to have
been thus introduced. That is a loose
method of reasoning, and if it were applied
all along the line of Hamlet it would produce singular results.

Wilson Barrett seems to suppose that if
the text be altered at points relative to
Hamlet's age, all discrepancies must disappear. That is anything but true. Indeed there is scarcely one of Shakespeare's
plays that is either free, or could be freed,
from discrepancies. Macbeth, for instance,
in the midst of one of his most essential
speeches, made at one of the most terrible
moments of his afflicted life, suddenly
ceases to talk like Macbeth and speaks in
what is instantly recognised as the characteristic voice of Shakespeare — introducing the simile of the poor player. In
Macbeth, also, cannon and dollars are an-

ticipated. In *King Lear* there is a mention of men who did not live till long after Lear's time. In *A Winter's Tale* occurs a shipwreck on the sea-coast of Bohemia — which has no sea-coast. In *Hamlet* we come upon the University of Wittenberg, an institution that did not exist until 1502, long after the period to which the story of the tragedy is supposed to relate. In *Hamlet*, also, ordnance is shot off — although in the historic age of that tragedy cannon had not been invented. Briefly, everything in the play is consonant not with the period of its historic basis but with the period of its authorship. One of the speeches in it, — one upon which Wilson Barrett especially relies to prove Hamlet's juvenility,

> "Think it no more,
> For nature, crescent, does not grow alone
> In thews and bulk, —

is put into the mouth of Laertes, a commonplace, shallow, and treacherous young man, to whose mind its lofty sentiment and philosophic beauty are alien. There again it is the poet who speaks, and not the dramatic individual. Shakespeare was a great poet as well as a great play-maker, and there are times when the copious flow of his poetic inspiration deranges the adjustment of details in the construction of his plays. Artistic consistency and symmetry, indeed, were not wilfully neglected by him. In essential things his plays are coherent and harmonious. But he did not care for pedantic accuracy ; and when his royal soul overflowed, as it often did, he heeded not through whose lips the golden torrent might break.

That Hamlet is to be regarded as a youth Wilson Barrett chiefly deduces from the fact that his mother, Queen Gertrude, is young enough for an amour with her husband's brother, Claudius. He would have the queen about thirty-six years old, instead of about forty-eight or fifty. Hamlet is not young enough to suit his theory at thirty, but the queen would be young enough to suit it at thirty-six, and therefore she must not have an adult son. He sees no difficulty in the way of making a youth of eighteen the natural exponent and voice of an embittered experience, a fatal grief, and a majestic contemplative philosophy, such as never yet was or could be possible to boyhood ; but he sees an insurmountable difficulty in the way of making an elderly woman lapse from virtue — at the solicitation of a lover, obviously younger than herself, who is completely infatuated about her — and this notwithstanding she is drawn as soft, sensuous, and vain, and is distinctly rebuked by her son, who should know her tolerably well, with conduct utterly inexplicable and senseless at a time of her life when

" The heyday in the blood is tame, it's humble,
    And waits upon the judgment."

He omits even to reflect that the amour of Gertrude and Claudius may have been going on for a long time prior to the murder of King Hamlet. Surely it is more probable that a well-preserved and handsome woman of forty-eight or fifty, weary of her too excellent husband and flattered by the passion of a desperate wooer, — who thought her so conjunctive to his life and soul that he could no more live without her than a star could move outside of its sphere, — should be an amatory sinner than it is that a lad of eighteen should be the mature philosopher, the profound moralist, the representative thinker, the grief-stricken, isolated sufferer, the intellectual, passionate, deep-hearted, supreme man whom Shakespeare has incarnated in Hamlet.

In all representations of *Hamlet* the
main thing is, and should be, Hamlet himself. The accessories are subordinated in
the piece, and they should be kept subordi-
nate in the presentment. Wilson Barrett's
effort so to assort the ages of the several
characters that the amatory relationship of
Claudius and Gertrude may impress his
mind as more rational and probable is not,
perhaps, unnatural. Hamlet himself considered that attachment preposterous —
saying to his mother, "At your age you
cannot call it love." But the brisk actor's
effort was an example of misdirected zeal.
Nobody cares much about Claudius and
Gertrude. Their story, and indeed the
story of the play, in so far as it relates to
merely mundane affairs, is one that lacks
absorbing interest. The essential substance
being the spiritual personality of Hamlet,
when an actor undertakes that part the
principal end that it concerns him to accomplish is the revelation of Hamlet's soul
and not the detail of his environment in
the Court of Denmark. The adjuncts
should be appropriate and the environment
should be harmonious — for all this helps
to preserve an illusion ; but all this will
not avail, unless the actor is able, by virtue

of the sovereign quality of his nature, to reach the height of the great argument and embody a true ideal of Shakespeare's conception.

But, even admitting that thirty is not young (whereas, in fact, it is), and that "young Hamlet" ought to be figured as a lad of eighteen, what good comes of it? Wherein is the observer enabled, by that means, to bring the experience and signification of Hamlet into a more intimate relationship with his own soul? Practically, Wilson Barrett — who did not and could not look or act like a boy — presented him as a full-grown, rather athletic man, trying to make himself boyish by acting in an alert manner. Were the actor to succeed, however, in substituting boy for man, he would still be bound to play the part according to the configuration and substance of it, as those are found in Shakespeare's tragedy. The essence of Hamlet is corrosive misery, and whether it be misery aged eighteen or misery aged thirty, the personality remains the same. Call him what age you will, his words, his conduct, and his nature remain unchanged. The mystery that enshrouds Hamlet, — a mystery that no order of mind, however lofty or

low, has ever analysed or ever will, — is
not that of an inscrutable individuality but
that of the agonised and half-insane condition of a royal and supreme soul overwhelmed with afflicting consciousness of
man's inexplicable and awful spiritual relation to the universe. Nothing could be
more obvious than the drift of the play;
nothing more distinct than the image of its
central character; and from the conditions
of that character, no matter what portal
of theory be opened, there is no escape.
Much has been said about the limit of
Hamlet's "madness." Much, at one time,
was said about the colour of his hair. It
is consistent with usage that there should
come a season of quibbling on the subject
of his age. By and by, perhaps, there will
arise a serious question as to the length of
his nose. Such considerations are imma-
terial. Call him a lad, if you like. It is
nonsense, but it does no harm — because,
practically, it can have no result. Your
nomination of him carries with it no warrant to turn him into a hobble-de-hoy, to
make him roll a hoop or spin a top, to
endue him with the agility of Jack-in-the-
Box, to lower a beautiful poetic conception
to the level of a peevish, petulant, froward
school-boy.

In Wilson Barrett's performance of Hamlet the manifestation of filial love was conspicuous for fervency and zeal. But filial love is not the sovereign charm of Hamlet, nor is it the dominant impulse of his character — an over-freighted, discordant harmony of all lovable qualities being the one, and the "scruple of thinking too precisely on the event" being the other. Filial he is, and filial love is a sweet and tender emotion; but a man may be an affectionate and devoted son without being, for that reason, an object of especial interest to the world. Venerable age overwhelmed with misery is exceedingly pathetic; but many a father is abused by his children without therefore becoming an image of the colossal majesty and ruined grandeur of King Lear. Any old man who is the victim of ingratitude and cruelty is an object of pity; but Lear's experience is possible only to Lear's nature; and, unless that nature be embodied, the picture of that experience can produce no adequate effect. The world does not love Hamlet because Hamlet loves his father, but because he is Hamlet.

Wilson Barrett transposed the soliloquy on death from the third act into the second. He preferred "a siege of troubles" to "a

sea" of them — as Edwin Forrest did,
long ago. He referred to a "k*i*ndless villain," not a kyndless one. He addressed
the greater part of "To be or not to be"
to the circumambient air — a region toward
which no human being ever gazes when his
mind is deeply absorbed in rumination.
In the parting scene with Ophelia he
caused Hamlet to make a spasmodic discovery of the furtive king, and immediately thereafter, a spasmodic discovery of
the furtive Polonius — each distinct. He
indicated Hamlet, at the close of that parting scene, as being so passionately attracted toward Ophelia that it is only by a
tremendous effort of the will that he can
break away from her; that being, manifestly, as false a touch as perverse ingenuity could put upon a mood that incarnates
the holiness and pathetic majesty of self-
renunciation. He placed the strongest possible emphasis upon Hamlet's hatred and
defiance of King Claudius — making the
prince so resolute and violent in that ani-
mosity that he was left without a reason
for not having at once accomplished his
revenge. He cut the king out of "No, his
affections do not that way tend," and he
closed act third with the queen's explana-

tion of the closet scene to her husband,
and with the business of despatching Hamlet to England. He laid a marked stress
upon Hamlet's "I essentially am not in
madness, but mad in craft," seeming to
suppose that this, absolutely and finally,
settles the question of Hamlet's insanity —
whereas this is, perhaps, the most characteristic denotement of mental aberration
that occurs in the tragedy. Persons who
have been shocked and dazed and who,
while not wholly unbalanced, know themselves to be queer, are sure, sooner or later,
to make a point of asserting their perfect
sanity. The most interesting of his restorations, and indeed the only important one,
was that of the passage in which Hamlet in
his delirium weeps over the body of Ophelia's father, whom, in his half frantic
mood, he has slain. "I'll lug the guts
into the neighbour room" was not spoken;
but it ought to be if this scene is to be
acted at all, in order to give the situation
its rightful effect. Hamlet has here become entirely wild, and he breaks down
in a paroxysm of mad, hysterical grief.
Wilson Barrett, at that point, and at the
exit after the play-scene [although there
the action of striking with a sword at imag-

inary, lurking foes was extravagant and
tended to lower the tone of the situation],
came more near to being Hamlet than anywhere else along the whole line of his performance. Everybody in the piece who
had to call Hamlet "young" or a "youth"
seemed to have been instructed to vocifer-
ate the juvenile designation, as with a
trumpet; but the king's line, "How dangerous is it that this man goes loose," was
merely murmured. Such were the peculiar
views and embellishments that, — with laborious effort and hard and brittle elocution,
— Wilson Barrett displayed as Hamlet.

At the zenith of his intellectual greatness,
the summit alike of his maturity and his
fame, and after studying and acting Hamlet for more than thirty years, that great
actor, Macready, — a wonderful man, to
whom the attribute of genius has been unjustly denied, by most of modern criticism,
for no better reason than because he was
scrupulously thorough, elaborate, methodi-
cal, and exacting as an artistic executant, —
wrote thus of Hamlet : "It seems to me as
if only now, at fifty-one years of age, I
thoroughly see and appreciate the artistic
power of Shakespeare in this great human
phenomenon ; nor do any of the critics,

Goethe, Schlegel, Coleridge, present to me, in their elaborate remarks, the exquisite artistical effects which I see in this work, as long meditation, like long straining after light, gives the minutest portion of its excellence to my view." A remark of kindred significance was made by Betterton, who, at the age of seventy, said to a friend who had praised his performance of Hamlet as "perfect" : "Perfect? I have played Hamlet now fifty years, and I believe I have not got to the depths of all its philosophy yet." Wilson Barrett, comparatively a beginner in Hamlet [his Young Prince was first exhibited in 1884], would appear to be troubled with no such scruples. "I have," he declared, "seen Hamlet played by every actor who has made a name in that character during the last twenty-five years. I know all their business and all their traditions. . . . When I made up my mind to produce the play in the Princess' theatre in London, I took up the book to study it, to try to improve on my old performance of the part, and as I read and studied I began to realise slowly how mistaken I had been. . . . For two years I worked on the play, analysing every line and every word. I arrived at my conclusions after years of study, and the character I have conceived is supported by some of the brightest intellects of our time. This is the outcome of a sincere conviction that I am absolutely right."

One of those intellects is Clement Scott, a learned, accomplished, competent, and expert dramatic critic. Mr. Scott wrote of Wilson Barrett's Hamlet, in an elaborate paper on that subject, these words: "I did not find tenderness, inspiration, or imagination." What remains in a personation of Hamlet from which those attributes are absent?

XXVIII.

TENNYSON.[1]

TENNYSON is dead. The best of all the poets since Byron has ended his career. He dies at a great age, passing away in his eighty-third year — a noble mission completed and a beautiful life fulfilled. That mission was to develop in himself great character and soul, and, by means of their perfect expression, in the finest and the most victorious form of art, to aid humanity in the achievement of spiritual progress. Most of the poets have perished prematurely. To Tennyson was allotted ample time. He attained, under the happiest conditions, to a full development and maturity. He has not left unsaid anything that it was within his power to express. Sorrow for his death

[1] This article was written by me in the *New York Tribune* of October 7, 1892, the morning after the death of Alfred, Lord Tennyson. It is, by request, included in this volume as a companion piece to the paper on Tennyson's play of *The Foresters*, in the first volume of this series.

is natural and it will be universal. He
was deeply loved and he will be long
and tenderly mourned. But sorrow for a
bereavement so obviously inevitable will
be chastened by the remembrance that in
a mortal condition of being there was nothing left for him to do, and that his release
— worn as he was and burdened with years
— must have come to him as a kindness
and a blessing. To the home that is darkened thousands of hearts, all over the
world, will send their silent tribute of
sympathy; but, outside of the poet's immediate circle of friends — conscious now
only of their personal affliction — the supreme feeling is that of grateful pride in the
majesty and purity of his character, in the
splendid affluence of his genius, and in the
permanence of his fame.

The worth and the rank of other poets,
in this generation, are disputed and discussed; but the worth and rank of Tennyson are not questioned. Such a fact is not
without its special significance. The word
of a poet is precious precisely in so far as it
expresses, not his heart alone, but the heart
that is universal — the passion, the emotion, the essential life of humanity at its
best. A word that is said for the hour

disappears with the hour for which it is
said, but when the soul of nature has
spoken, its message becomes an essential
part of human experience and dwells in the
memory forever. Tennyson is the poet of
love and of sorrow, of passion and of affection, of pageantry and of pathos, of sublim-
ity and of faith ; and especially he is the
poet of destiny and of will. The range of
his vision is very broad. His glance is
penetrating and deep. His voice is not the
echo of the age in which he lived — however he may have been disturbed by the
conflicts of that age — but it is a voice
proceeding out of the elemental source of
things and uttering absolute truth in words
that are beautiful, and final, and perfect.
The reader of Tennyson finds that his own
spirit — his essential experience, his discontent, his aspiration, the inmost fibre of his
being — is expressed for him, with a fulness, a passionate sincerity, and an artistic
beauty that he could never hope to reach,
and that satisfy him fully, and lead, and
guide, and strengthen him. The human
mind — glad and thankful in the presence
of much good, but not blind to the existence of much evil — has never yet succeeded in proving that everything will

finish well, nor has it ever yet succeeded
in illuminating the way in which that consummation is to be obtained. Nevertheless it believes in the ultimate triumph of
good. That conviction is adamantine in
the poetry of Tennyson. His distinctive
note, undoubtedly, is the pathetic note. "I
shall never see thee more, in the long gray
fields, at night." The evanescence of man
and of all his works is steadily present,
and even when the trumpets are at their
loudest the low sob of the organ is heard,
in its solemn undertone of warning and
of lament. Yet this is a poet who rests
calmly on the strength of human will and
looks without fear into the eyes of death.
Such a poet is a leader and a comforter of
the race, and it is right and natural that he
should have its love and homage.

The thoroughness and the wise, far-
sighted patience with which Tennyson
developed his mind and ascertained and
exercised his poetic faculties offer a lesson
of supreme value in the conduct of intellectual life. No one of the poets has manifested more — few authors, whether poets
or not, have manifested so much — of the
grand stability that consists in sane con-
tinence and poise. With Tennyson genius

was not delirium. His works give no sign
of that feverish straining after effect, that
strenuous reaching upward for an object or
an idea, that flurry of wild endeavour and
painful and abortive fuss, which are characteristic of a petty mind. He was born
great, but he so nurtured and trained and
disciplined his powers that he steadily in-
creased in greatness. He made his intellect broad and he kept it holy, in order that
the revelations of nature and of the spiritual world might flow through it as through
their rightful channel. He was not warped
from his true course by the influence of
other men or by any consideration of popular applause and of the idle fancies and
fleeting caprice of mankind. He was not
that sentimental and effusive demagogue,
the poet of the people; he was something
far higher and better than that — he was
the poet of man. Like Wordsworth —
his illustrious predecessor, with whom, in
the attribute of stately individuality and
the circumstance of temperamental isolation, he was kindred — he took his own
path. There was once a time when Tennyson received little but ridicule and
neglect; and then presently came a time
when he received an homage amounting to

idolatry; but during neither of those periods
was his serenity disturbed. The ideal of
lofty, inflexible character and pure and
perfect manliness that his poetry continually presents was the unconscious reflex
of himself. His magnificent ode on the
death of the Duke of Wellington, one of
the best poems in the language, thrills and
trembles with profound and passionate exultation in the reality of virtuous strength
and moral grandeur. Such as King Arthur
is, in his immortal pages, so was the poet
in life; and the shining words of Shakespeare might always have been used to
denote him:

"Like a great sea-mark, standing every flaw,
     And saving those that eye thee."

The transcendent attributes of power that
his works disclose are the heart and the
imagination. Their vitality of feeling —
never shown in discord or tumult, but always present, like the central heat of the
sun — is colossal; and, looking back upon
the current of his years and the incessant
fertility of his achievement, it is nothing
less than marvellous that such intense
emotion should have kept itself alive in
that poet for so long a time. He wrote,

indeed, a few weak things toward the last; but almost till the end his voice was a clarion and his pen was fire. In his poem of *Locksley Hall Sixty Years After* there is the same strain of noble and impassioned feeling — loftier, grander, more predominant and more august, if anything — that burns in the *Locksley Hall* of his vigorous and splendid youth. He needed not to go out of himself for his inspiration. The flame leaped from within. The altar was never darkened and never cold. Every influence that experience and the environment of his life could liberate became tremulous with sensibility and eloquent with divine meaning the moment it touched his mind. It was as if the wandering breeze derived warmth and fragrance and endless melody from only sweeping the strings of the harp that had been placed to receive its caress. He was an example, furthermore, of that miracle of nature, the renewal of the elemental poetic power. At a time when it seemed, with the death of Byron, that the last poetic voice was hushed, and that no word more could ever be said, suddenly the genius of Tennyson sprang into light, and the world was dowered with a literature of poetry essentially and abso-

lutely new. The poetry of Tennyson, while
never eccentric, is unique. It has indeed
been widely imitated — as he himself observed, when he said that "Most can raise
the flower now, for all have got the seed."
But the hand of the master remains un-
rivalled. The blank verse of Tennyson
possesses a rich quality of music and an
indescribable potency of movement that
were his own. He used many of the old
forms of versification, but he beautified
every one of them that he touched. The
stanza of *In Memoriam* occurs in Ben Jonson; but Tennyson gave it a grace and
flexibility and copious and sonorous music,
far beyond Jonson's reach. In the inven-
tion of new forms he was remarkably ingenious, but it is notable — as in *The Lotos
Eaters*, *The Two Voices*, *Margaret*, and
many more — that with Tennyson the
form is always the inevitable sequence
of the thought. Every fibre of his art was
pervaded with inspiration. He has shown
that the most delicate and beautiful refinement of mechanism, in the use of language,
is not incompatible with boundless feeling.
He has made intolerable and impossible
henceforth, in poetry, the bad extremes of
tumid verbiage and of soulless form. Alike

to literature and to life the services that
Tennyson has rendered are those of perpetual blessing, and the world is nobler and
better, and the life of coming generations
will be sweeter and more beautiful, because
he has lived and written.

THE WORKS OF

WILLIAM WINTER.

SHAKESPEARE'S ENGLAND. 18MO, CLOTH, 75 CENTS.

GRAY DAYS AND GOLD. 18MO, CLOTH, 75 CENTS.

SHADOWS OF THE STAGE. 18MO, CLOTH, 75 CENTS.

SHADOWS OF THE STAGE. Second Series. 18MO, CLOTH, 75 CENTS.

OLD SHRINES AND IVY. 18MO, CLOTH, 75 CENTS.

Also a Small Limited LARGE PAPER EDITION. 4 Vols. Uniform. $8.00.

WANDERERS: A Collection of Poems. NEW EDITION. WITH A PORTRAIT. 18MO, CLOTH, 75 CENTS.

"The supreme need of this age in America is a practical conviction that progress does not consist in material prosperity, but in spiritual advancement. Utility has long been exclusively worshipped. The welfare of the future lies in the worship of beauty. To that worship these pages are devoted, with all that implies of sympathy with the higher instincts, and faith in the divine destiny of the human race." — *From the Preface to Gray Days and Gold.*

MACMILLAN & CO.,

112 FOURTH AVENUE, NEW YORK.

SHADOWS OF THE STAGE.

18MO, CLOTH, 75 CENTS.

"The fame of the actor more than that of any other artist is an evanescent one—a 'bubble reputation'—indeed, and necessarily so from the conditions under which his genius is exercised. While the impression it makes is often more vivid and inspiring for the moment than that of the poet and the painter, it vanishes almost with the occasion which gave it birth, and lives only as a tradition in the memory of those to whom it had immediately appealed. 'Shadows they are, and shadows they pursue.'

"The writer, therefore, who, gifted with insight and a poetic enthusiasm which enables him to discern on the one hand the beauties in a dramatic work not perceived by the many, and on the other the qualities in the actor which have made him a true interpreter of the poet's thought, at the same time possessing the faculty of revealing to us felicitously the one, and the other is certainly entitled to our grateful recognition.

"Such a writer is Mr. William Winter, easily the first,—for we know of none other living in this country, or in the England he loves so much, in whose nature the critic's vision is united with that of the poet so harmoniously. . . .

"Over and above all this, there is in these writings the same charm of style, poetic glamour and flavor of personality which distinguish whatever comes to us from Mr. Winter's pen, and which make them unique in our literature."—*Home Journal*, New York.

MACMILLAN & CO.,

112 FOURTH AVENUE, NEW YORK.

OLD SHRINES AND IVY.

18MO, CLOTH, 75 CENTS.

CONTENTS.

SHRINES OF HISTORY.

SHRINES OF LITERATURE.

"Whatever William Winter writes is marked by felicity of diction and by refinement of style, as well as by the evidence of culture and wide reading. 'Old Shrines and Ivy' is an excellent example of the charm of his work."— *Boston Courier.*

MACMILLAN & CO.,

112 FOURTH AVENUE,   NEW YORK.

(4)

SHAKESPEARE'S ENGLAND.

18MO, CLOTH, 75 CENTS.

" . . . It was the author's wish, in dwelling thus upon the rural loveliness, and the literary and historical associations of that delightful realm, to afford sympathetic guidance and useful suggestion to other American travellers who, like himself, might be attracted to roam among the shrines of the mother-land. Temperament is the explanation of style; and he has written thus of England because she has filled his mind with beauty and his heart with mingled joy and sadness; and surely some memory of her venerable ruins, her ancient shrines, her rustic glens, her gleaming rivers, and her flower-spangled meadows will mingle with the last thoughts that glimmer through his brain when the shadows of the eternal night are falling and the ramble of life is done." — *From the Preface.*

"He offers something more than guidance to the American traveller. He is a convincing and eloquent interpreter of the august memories and venerable sanctities of the old country." — *Saturday Review.*

"The book is delightful reading." — *Scribner's Monthly.*

"Enthusiastic and yet keenly critical notes and comments on English life and scenery." — *Scotsman.*

MACMILLAN & CO.,

112 FOURTH AVENUE,   NEW YORK.

(5)

GRAY DAYS
AND GOLD.

18MO, CLOTH, 75 CENTS.

CONTENTS.

This book, which is intended as a companion to *Shakespeare's England*, relates to the gray days of an American wanderer in the British Isles, and to the gold of thought and fancy that can be found there.

MACMILLAN & CO.,

112 FOURTH AVENUE, NEW YORK.